CITIZENSHIP
EDUCATION FOR KS3

JULIA FIEHN

TERRY FIEHN

HODDER
EDUCATION
AN HACHETTE UK COMPANY

The publisher would like to thank the following for permission to reproduce copyright material:

Photo credits

p.54 © Barry Batchelor/PA Archive/Press Association Images; **p.55** © Andrew Aitchison / Alamy; **p.61** *tl* © ullsteinbild / TopFoto, *tr* Reproduced with kind permission of Bristol Pound CIC; **p.68** © antbphotos – Fotolia; **p.69** © Getty Images/iStockphoto; **p.83** © Alfredo Estrella/AFP/Getty Images; **p.89** *r* ©TopFoto/Topham Picturepoint, *bl* LC-USZC4-5321/Library of Congress Rare Book and Special Collections Division Washington, D.C. 20540 USA, *br* © Evening Standard/Hulton Archive/ Getty Images; **p.90** © Andrew Burton/Getty Images; **p.95** *br* http://commons.wikimedia.org/wiki/ File%3APassing_of_the_Parliament_Bill%2C_1911_-_Project_Gutenberg_eText_19609.jpg, *ml* http://www.flickr.com/photos/trialsanderrors/4366952415/; *tr* © Imagestate Media (John Foxx); **p.96** *tr, mr, bl* © Rex Features, *br* © Maciej Zych – Fotolia; **p.97** *tl, mr, br*, ©Rex Features, *ml* ©Tim Rooke/ Rex Features, *bl* © Getty Images; **p.106** Logos reproduced by permission of the Animal Welfare Party, Conservative Party, DUP, Green Party, Labour Party, Liberal Democrat Party, Libertarian Party UK, Monster Raving Loony Party, NLP, Plaid Cymru; Respect Party, SDLP, Sinn Fein, SNP, UKIP, UUP; **p.116** ©Vit Kovalcik – Fotolia; **p.118** © Lisa Ryder / Alamy; **p.120** *bl* Reproduced with the kind permission of the British Medical Association, *bm* © We Made This Ltd, *br* Reproduced with the kind permission of Forest; **p.122** Reproduced with the kind permission of 38 Degrees.

Text acknowledgements

p.17 'No man is an island' by John Donne; **p.28** Grateful thanks to the staff and pupils of Bishop's Hatfield Girls' School and especially to Sue Carter; **p.35** Permission for re-use of all © Crown copyright information is granted under the terms of the Open Government Licence (OGL); **p.43** quotes adapted from Wasted Lives by Mark Liddle, National Association for the Care and Resettlement of Offenders (NACRO) (November, 1998); **p.59** 'Restorative Justice for Offenders', by Restoraive Solutions CIC, http://www.restorativesolutions.org.uk/page/104/Offenders.htm; **p.90** Copyright Guardian News & Media Ltd 2013.

Every effort has been made to trace all copyright holders, but if any have been inadvertently overlooked the Publishers will be pleased to make the necessary arrangements at the first opportunity.

Although every effort has been made to ensure that website addresses are correct at time of going to press, Hodder Education cannot be held responsible for the content of any website mentioned in this book. It is sometimes possible to find a relocated web page by typing in the address of the home page for a website in the URL window of your browser.

Hachette UK's policy is to use papers that are natural, renewable and recyclable products and made from wood grown in sustainable forests. The logging and manufacturing processes are expected to conform to the environmental regulations of the country of origin.

Orders: please contact Bookpoint Ltd, 130 Milton Park, Abingdon, Oxon OX14 4SB. Telephone: +44 (0)1235 827720. Fax: +44 (0)1235 400454. Lines are open 9.00a.m.–5.00p.m., Monday to Saturday, with a 24-hour message answering service. Visit our website at www.hoddereducation.co.uk

© Julia Fiehn, Terry Fiehn 2014
First published in 2014 by
Hodder Education,
An Hachette UK Company
Carmelite House, 50 Victoria Embankment, London EC4Y 0DZ

Impression number 10 9 8 7 6 5 4
Year   2019 2018 2017

Cover photo © Tim Ellis / Alamy

Illustrations © Peter Lubach; © Barking Dog
Typeset in 11/14 Frutiger LT Std 45 Light by Integra Software Services Pvt. Ltd., Pondicherry, India
Printed in Dubai
A catalogue record for this title is available from the British Library

ISBN 9781471806940

Introduction

Citizenship Education is an important part of the development of young people. It aims to encourage them to participate in decision-making, firstly within their own social groups and their school, and later on in their communities. The strength and development of our democracy relies on people participating at a local and national level, and especially by voting in elections. Young people need to develop an interest in the way decisions are made and consider how they themselves can influence decisions, if they are to take part when they are older. The activities in this book are designed to encourage them to develop this interest and equip them with the understanding and skills to participate effectively, as well as pass on relevant knowledge about our democratic system of government.

This book is divided into six sections which cover the Citizenship Programme of Study for KS3.

Rules, fairness, rights and responsibilities
Communities and identities
Laws and the justice system
Managing money
Liberty and freedom
Parliamentary democracy

The sections are self-contained units. Teachers should choose the topics and activities in each section that fit in with their own programmes of work and suit the needs of their pupils.

Contents

1.1 The Excellent Community School

Activity

You are a group of local people who have decided to set up and run a small new community school, called the Excellent Community School. There's a lot to do, but now you are at the stage of writing the school rules and deciding on the discipline policy. Work in pairs.

1 Choose three areas of school life from the following list and write the school rules that should apply to these areas. The rules could be very different from your own school, or they could be the same.

- Uniform
- Homework
- Behaviour in class
- Behaviour in the playground and corridors
- Bullying
- Lateness
- Attendance
- School equipment

2 When you have finished, find a pair who wrote rules for at least one of the same areas as you. Compare the two sets of rules and try to agree on amendments.

3 Now move on to work with another pair and do the same thing with rules on another area of school life.

4 Share all the rules written by the whole class and discuss whether they are fair.

Punishments

Most groups enforce the rules through bad consequences for those who break them. In schools, these punishments are often detention, letters home or withdrawal of privileges, but how the punishments are given out can vary from school to school.

Activity

There is some disagreement between the people setting up the Excellent Community School about discipline policy. The two opposing views are described in the boxes below. What are your views of each policy? Discuss the following questions:

- Which system of rules and punishments is fairest? Why?

- Which system do you think would be the most effective?

- Which system is most like your own school?

- If you don't like either system, write a box yourself, describing what you think is fair.

The firm but fair school

- Discipline should be firm and predictable. No excuses will be tolerated.

- Every class will have a list of rules pinned to the wall and each offence will be given a number of points.

- A prefect in every class will have the job of reporting rule-breakers to the teacher.

- When a pupil has collected a certain number of points in one term, there will be a set punishment.

The punishments will be:
2 points: Writing a letter of apology to the teacher.
4 points: Standing in the middle of the stage during daily assembly.
6 points: Detention for 30 minutes after school.
10 points: Detention for one hour after school and a letter home.
15 points: Exclusion for one day.
20 points: Exclusion for a week.
30 points: Expulsion.

The reasonable school

- Discipline should be reasonable and flexible.

- Pupils will vote on the rules they would like in the school.

- Pupils who break a rule will firstly be interviewed by their form teacher. If the teacher believes that there was no good reason for the rule-breaking, the pupil will be sent to the head of year in order to explain his/her behaviour.

- If the pupil misbehaves again in the same week, the elected school council will consider what should happen to the pupil, listen to his/her side of the argument and decide on the punishment.

- For repeated offences, a school disciplinary council – the head, deputy head, a parent and two pupils – will sit to decide what should be done with the pupil.

- Punishments might consist of collecting litter in the playground, sweeping out the classrooms or doing some other job around the school.

1.2 Rules

All groups develop rules – things you can and can't do. They should apply equally to all group members, no matter how strong or powerful or privileged some of them are. If this doesn't happen, then we say that the rules are unfair, and fairness is very important to all of us.

Families usually have their own rules, and so do friendship groups, youth clubs, schools and workplaces. Some of the rules are formal and written down. Others are informal, but are still clearly understood by all members of the group. There are usually consequences for those who break the rules. Schools have formal, written rules that aim to keep order and protect everyone in the school.

Activity

As a whole class, discuss your school rules.

1 Which ones do you think are fair and which are unfair?

2 Which ones would you change if you could?

3 What are the punishments that are most often used in your school when pupils break the rules?

4 In pairs, discuss six rules that you think a school must have.

5 For each rule, decide what punishment a pupil should receive for breaking it and explain what the punishment should achieve.

- NO RUNNING IN CORRIDOR -

Make your own ground rules for discussions

Usually in classroom discussions, when there is disagreement, lots of people try to talk at the same time. If everyone shouts and interrupts, no-one can hear other people's viewpoints, and no-one learns anything new. So you need ground rules that everybody has to follow and the best way to make sure everyone follows them is to make the rules yourselves.

NO EATING IN THE CLASSROOM

STATEMENT STARTERS

A 'When we are discussing as a class, we should ...'

B 'When someone is talking, we should ...'

C 'If someone disagrees with what someone else has said ...'

D 'If there are different views in the class, we could ...'

E 'Decisions could be made by ...'

F 'If we don't understand what someone has said, we should ...'

G 'If someone breaks the rules ...'

H 'If someone is unkind ...'

Activity

1 Working in pairs, draw up your list of rules. You can use the 'Statement Starters' on the right if you like.

2 When you have finished, join up with another pair, share what you have written and try to come to some agreement on your list of rules.

3 All the pairs should then come together as a class and agree the set of rules.

4 Make posters of the agreed rules to display around the class.

1.3 It's not fair! Applying the rules

People sometimes say 'It's not fair' when they mean 'I don't like the way I am being treated'. It is important to understand what fairness is when decisions are to be made about applying rules. Most of us like to think that we are fair to other people and we want to be treated fairly ourselves. We could say that, in order to be fair when applying rules, we must:

- treat people equally
- not favour particular people
- not discriminate against particular people
- be sure about the facts of the case
- make sure that the punishment is not too harsh or too lenient.

It is not quite so easy applying rules as it might appear. It can be difficult to be fair to everyone. Look at Robert Simpson's day as a teacher and all the things he has to deal with. Could you do better?

Activity

Work in pairs. Read what Robert Simpson did through the day. Whenever he made a decision, you have to decide whether he was right, partly right or wrong. Be prepared to say why and what you would have done.

Robert Simpson arrived just on time for school as he had been up part of the night with his new baby. However, Tom Drake in his tutor group had not arrived on time again. He knew that Tom had a difficult journey by bus, but the head teacher had recently stressed that there could be no excuses for being late.

Decision 1
He gave Tom a late detention.

At registration Vanita told him that she had forgotten to bring her money for the trip to the rap music session that all the pupils had been looking forward to.

Decision 2
He said that Vanita could not go. Vanita was upset and said she would bring the money the next day, but Mr Simpson said he would stick to his decision.

After registration Robert went off to teach his first lesson, an English GCSE class. As he was talking to the class, he spotted Jason tweeting on his mobile phone.

Decision 3
He took Jason's phone away and said he would give it to the head of year. One of Jason's parents would have to come to the school to collect it. It was a strict rule of the school that mobile phones should not be used in lessons.

Fortunately the next lesson passed without incident and Robert went off to get a cup of tea at break-time. As he came round the corner, he saw an older boy pinning a younger one against the wall. The younger one appeared to be crying. He questioned them about what they were doing, but they said they were just mucking around.

Decision 4
He decided to do nothing and went off to have his cup of tea.

In the last lesson before lunch, his Year 7 class kept on being noisy. Some of the pupils were making noises when his back was turned, but he could not pin down who the troublemakers were. After one warning …

Decision 5
He told them he would keep them in for 10 minutes at lunch and add on 5 minutes if the disturbance happened again. It did, so he kept them for 15 minutes even though the pupils complained that they would lose their place in the dinner queue and there would not be much left.

Robert Simpson grabbed a quick lunch and got his lesson materials ready for the afternoon. Afternoon registration was quick and easy. But the first lesson with his Year 9 English class did not go so smoothly. In the middle of the lesson Nissa Ahmed suddenly jumped up and threw her schoolbag at Jake Jenks, hitting him in the face. She said that he had made a racist statement about her family and religious beliefs.

Decision 6
Mr Simpson hauled Jake out of the class and sent him to the deputy head teacher, who deals with racist incidents. Jake was sent home with a letter to his parents at the end of the afternoon.

Robert Simpson was glad when the final school lesson bell sounded. It had been a long day.

Activity

1 How far did you agree with Mr Simpson's decisions?
2 What decisions did you find difficult?
3 Why do you think it is difficult to apply rules so that they are fair to everybody?

However, the rest of the class was unsettled. Some pupils told Mr Simpson that Jake did not make the remarks and that Nissa was angry with him because he had dumped her best friend and she wanted to get him into trouble.

Decision 7
Mr Simpson ignored their comments.

1.4 It's not fair! Who gets what?

People sometimes say 'It's not fair' when they mean 'I'm not getting what I want'. It is important to understand what fairness is when decisions are to be made about who gets what. The trouble is that it is not always easy to make a fair decision or to judge what is fair, and people often disagree about fairness. Every individual has rights, but some might have greater need or they might deserve more.

We could say that, in order to be fair, we must:

- treat people equally
- not favour particular people
- not discriminate against particular people
- think about the different circumstances people come from.

Activity

Look at the examples on this page and on page 13. Choose the option that you think is fairest in each case, but you will have to give reasons for your choice. You might be able to think of a fairer solution in each case.

Who goes on the trip?

The teacher could select:

A The pupils who have worked hardest during the whole year.

B The pupils who are having a bad time at school or home.

C The pupils who will behave best on the trip.

Dear Mr Simpson,

Thank you and Class 7S so much for the amazing fundraising you have done for our charity. We'd like to invite **TWO** representatives from the class to **CELEBRITY FEST** next month, the UK's biggest celebrity charity event.

Who gets the best bedroom?

The parent could:

A Give the best room to the oldest child.

B Give the best room to the most helpful child.

C Give six months in the room to each child.

THIS ONE IS <u>MY</u> ROOM!

The leg of the football table has broken.

Who pays?

The youth leader could:

A Ask the members to club together for a new one.

B Try to find out who did it and exclude that member from the club.

C Buy a new one from club funds instead of the promised trip to a bowling alley.

Who deserves to play?

The coach could:

A Give a chance to someone who hasn't played in the team yet.

B Select the player who always turns up for practice.

C Select the risky player who might score goals but also might commit fouls.

Who should represent us?

The pupils could vote for:

A The class member who is the most confident and speaks out well.

B The class member who promises to keep everyone informed.

C The class member who is the most popular.

Activity

Discuss the following questions:

1 Does everyone agree about the fairest solution in each case?

2 Which decisions were the most difficult?

3 Why do you think it is difficult to make decisions about who gets what?

1.5 What rights should all children have?

Children often feel that adults stop them from doing things they have a right to do. Adults say that they are protecting the child or looking after the child's interests.

Some adults think that children do not have rights at all and that they are not able to decide matters for themselves.

Activity

1 Think of two or three occasions when an adult stopped you doing something you felt you had a right to do. Discuss the events in class.

2 What rights should all children have? Read the speech bubbles on these pages with a partner.

Note down the rights that you think are really important. Note the ones you do not think are important or can't decide about. You could write them in a table like the one below: the first one has been done for you.

It is important that children should have the right to …	It is not important that children should have the right to …	Children should NOT have the right to …
A Free education		

A I should have the right to free education.

B I should have the right to go to bed when I want to.

C I should be able to get enough food to keep me healthy.

D I should have the right to stay with my family or the people who love me and want to look after me.

E I should have the right to drink alcohol.

F There should be times when I can play and relax.

G I should be able to go out and stay out until I decide it's time to come home.

H I should have the right to work to earn money to help my family.

I Adults should not bully me, beat me or abuse me in any way.

J Adults should listen to my views when they make a decision that will affect my life.

K I should have the right to eat sweets when I want to.

L I should have the right to decide what I learn at school.

M I should have the right to special care and education if I am disabled.

N I should have the right to watch whatever I like online.

O I should be allowed to develop my abilities and talents to the fullest.

P I should have the right to use a credit card.

Activity

Discuss these questions:
1. Which rights were you not sure about and why?
2. Which did you think were really important rights?
3. Which were not so important?
4. Which should children *not* have a right to?
5. Which other rights would you add to the ones you have said were important?

1.6 What responsibilities do we have to each other?

People expect to have rights, but do they expect to have responsibilities? We all have a responsibility to make sure that we don't put ourselves and other people in danger. But what other kinds of responsibility do people have towards each other, and how do we decide which are the most important?

Activity

1 Think about the people on the list below. Who would come first for you if they were in difficulty? Put the list in order of your priority and explain your decisions.

Grandparents

Parents

Elderly people you don't know

Strangers of your own age

Teachers

Brothers/sisters

Yourself

Friends

Neighbours

People living far away in other countries

Activity

2 Now look at the situations below and on page 17. Would any of these change the way you think about your responsibilities to different people and the order you placed them in above?

You really want to buy a new CD, but you have been moved by the plight of people across the other side of the world involved in a terrible natural disaster. You could donate the money to help them.

Your friends have asked you to join them at a party. It will be a real laugh. However, it is your gran's 70th birthday and she is looking forward to seeing all of her family.

Your teacher is counting on you to help paint the set for the school production after school today. You are good at art, you like the teacher and you promised you would. However, your mum has been asked out for an early evening drink and says she needs you to look after your baby brother.

You are out with a group of friends when you meet a young boy that you don't know. One of your friends trips him up on purpose and he hurts his leg. His things spill out over the floor and all his money falls out of his pocket. Your friends walk off laughing, but the boy asks you for help.

Your older brother likes to tag walls. An elderly neighbour has just had a new garden wall built. He is really pleased with it and is not very well off. Your brother says he is going to spray the new wall with his tag. You could try to persuade him not to, since you and your brother get on very well.

You have seen a pair of trainers that you really like but you have also discovered that the people who make them work very long hours for little money. Do you refuse to buy the trainers and send a letter to the company to tell them why, or do you buy them and think it's only one pair and what you do does not make any difference?

Activity

1   How do we decide who to put first in difficult situations like these?
2   Why is it sometimes difficult to decide against our friends?
3   Do you think that you have any responsibility towards other people who you don't know?
4   What do you think the expression 'no man is an island' means? Do you agree with it?

No man is an island,
Entire of itself,
Each is a piece of the continent,
A part of the main.

John Donne (1572–1631)

How far should pupils have a say in what goes on in school?

Some people say that you learn useful skills and feel that you belong if you are allowed to voice your views and be listened to. Others think that children do not have enough experience of life to be able to influence important decisions.

Situations

The school is to have a new headteacher. The job has been advertised and people have applied.

Should pupils be involved in:
- shortlisting
- meeting applicants
- interviewing?

Dinner time at the school is very chaotic. Too many people are trying to pass through the dining hall in too short a time. Some Year 7 pupils have worked out a plan that might improve things.

Should the headteacher listen and be persuaded to try out the plan?

The school grounds are very scruffy, with litter blowing around, graffiti on the walls and nowhere to sit. Some money has been made available for improvements – new bins, a clean-up and some seating.

Should pupils be consulted about how the grounds can be kept in good condition?

There has always been a debate in the school about uniform. No-one likes the existing one – the colours are drab and the styles old-fashioned. Some people think there should be no uniform at all; others think the uniform should be re-designed.

Should pupils be involved in making the decision by debating and voting?

Some schools have elected an 'associate pupil governor' from amongst the pupils. The pupil does not have a vote, but attends meetings and listens. He/she is allowed to report some of the items (but not confidential ones) back to other pupils.

Should your school have an associate pupil governor?

The school is to be rebuilt on a new site and the new buildings will be opened in four years' time. There are some choices that have to be made about the improved facilities.

Should there be a pupil committee working with staff and the architect?

Skills

Listening to different points of view

Expressing a point of view and explaining it

Asking sensible questions and following up things you don't understand

Being able to say briefly what was said (summarising) and reporting back to others

Arguing a case

Speaking on behalf of others and putting their views even if you don't agree with them yourself

Negotiating – accepting compromises if reasonable

Finding out what other people think, and deciding what the majority view is

Making your views known

There are a number of different ways in which pupils can regularly make their views known and offer suggestions to change things:

- school councils
- suggestion boxes
- notice boards
- blogs on the school website
- school magazines
- focus groups (where small groups of pupils are consulted on specific issues)
- whole school votes, through a show of hands in assembly, or a referendum with votes being put in a ballot box
- discussing what is going to be learnt in subjects.

School councils

Many schools these days have some kind of school council, which is made up of elected pupil representatives. All the pupils in the school have the chance to stand for election to represent their class, their year group or their house.

School councils have a number of purposes:

- to help everyone in the school to feel responsible for what goes on there
- to improve relationships between teachers and pupils
- to help pupils get on better with each other
- to solve any problems in the school
- to build pupils' confidence by giving them a chance to speak in public
- to give pupils the skills needed to work in groups.

Activity

1 Do you have a school council in your school? If so, how is it organised?

2 How are members of the council selected? Do you think this is a fair way of choosing representatives?

3 Pick two of the 'purposes' of school councils that you think your council fulfils and say why.

The elected members of the council meet regularly, sometimes with a teacher present, and sometimes not. They discuss items that have been put on the agenda by pupils and staff. The council's decisions are written down and put forward to the head teacher, and sometimes the governors of the school.

School councils are run differently in different schools and some work better than others. Here are some of the criticisms pupils have made of school councils:

A *I'm not interested in the school council. It's boring and doesn't affect me.*

B *It's always the same kinds of pupils who get elected to the council – the clever and confident ones.*

C *Whatever the school council decides, the headteacher really makes the decisions. We can't change anything.*

D *We never hear what happens at council meetings. They don't tell the rest of us anything.*

E *The school council is a clique. They think they are the top dogs because the teachers consult them.*

F *I never manage to get my items on the agenda of the school council. Who decides what they talk about? Not me.*

Activity

1 Work in small groups and discuss each of the statements above. How far is each one true of your school council?

2 If some of the statements are true, what could be done to change things?

3 a Discuss your ideas as a class. Each group calls out one idea at a time. This should be written on the board. If an idea is put forward by more than one group, it should be ticked each time it is suggested.

b Pick the three ideas that have the most ticks and hold a vote on which improvement is the most important. You can suggest this improvement to your school council representative, or you could write a letter to the school council from the class, asking for your ideas to go on the next agenda.

1.8 Taking part in a debate

Debating is a good way to explore all sides of a particular issue. Usually the issue is put in the form of a statement that people can argue about, e.g. 'Pupils should be allowed to use smartphones in class.' We call this a motion.

In the picture, you can see the different roles people play in a debate. You are now going to debate the issue about smartphones. This is a good issue to discuss because we have been looking at fairness, rights, responsibilities and having a say. Children have rights, as you discussed on pages 14-15. But teachers are responsible for making sure pupils concentrate in class and learn well.

Activity

Arrange the classroom and agree the main speakers. Give them and others a chance to prepare their arguments. Use the statements here and on page 24 to get started. You could also do some research (see page 25).

I am arguing that it is obvious that pupils should be allowed to use smartphones in class. My reasons for saying this are …

Pupils need to learn to use all the information available in this modern world. Smartphones are here to stay.

The motion for the debate today is: 'This house believes that pupils should be allowed to use their smartphones in class.'

Chairperson

My role is to run and control the debate.
- I keep everybody in order.
- I start the debate by reading out the motion.
- I call people to speak and keep to time.
- I choose people from the audience to join in, taking people in turn for and against the motion.
- I try to make sure the debate is fair.
- At the end I take a vote on whether people are for or against the motion.

For the motion

Speaker 1

My role is to speak first FOR the motion.
- I make points to support the motion.
- I speak for 2–3 minutes.

Speaker 3
- I also speak for the motion.
- I speak for 2–3 minutes.

The audience

Against the motion

Speaker 2

My role is to speak first AGAINST the motion.
- I make points which disagree with the motion.
- I speak for 2–3 minutes.

Speaker 4

- I also speak against the motion.
- I speak for 2–3 minutes.

Our role is to listen and contribute to the debate.
- We listen to the speeches from both sides.
- We can ask the speakers questions.
- We can make our own short speeches or give our views.
- We can only join in when the chairperson says so.

Arguments for and against the motion: *Pupils should be allowed to use their smartphones in class.*

Arguments for

Arguments against

66 *Pupils need to be educated to take their places in the modern world. Smartphones are used all the time in the workplace.* 99

66 *Some pupils do not have smartphones or indeed any kind of mobile phone. Allowing pupils to use them gives those pupils an advantage.* 99

66 *The internet is an important source of information and pupils should be taught how to use it with discrimination. Smartphones provide access to the internet.* 99

66 *Pupils will not concentrate on the lesson if they are playing with their phones.* 99

66 *It is impossible to stop pupils using phones and confiscating them causes more headaches for teachers.* 99

66 *Some pupils will text, send photos or tweet about the lesson and this is wrong since other pupils or the teacher may be criticised.* 99

66 *Pupils have got used to rules about having phones turned off in class. It is healthy for them to learn to do without their phones while in lessons.* 99

66 *Many pupils have got used to having their phones with them. It is not right to remove their property against their wishes.* 99

Developing your debating skills

You can improve your debating skills by practising them regularly. Here are some areas to work on.

A Researching

You have to understand the issue you are debating. This means finding out about it – collecting information and evidence to use in the debate. You can find out what other people think about the issue with reasons to back up your opinions, plus evidence for your views. You can get information from a number of sources.

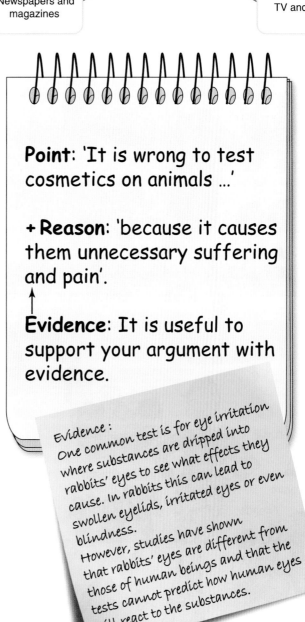

B Making points and giving reasons

In a debate you need to make points clearly and give reasons for your views, if possible with evidence. We call this making an argument. An example of this is on the right.

Activity

1. Give an example from the smartphones debate (pages 22–24) when someone made a point and gave a reason to back up the point.

2. Work in pairs. Come up with a point and a reason on each of the following topics:
   - All school meals should be free.
   - Children under 11 should not be out on the streets after 9pm without an adult.
   - Parents should not be allowed to smack their children at all.

Point: 'It is wrong to test cosmetics on animals ...'

+ Reason: 'because it causes them unnecessary suffering and pain'.

Evidence: It is useful to support your argument with evidence.

Evidence:
One common test is for eye irritation where substances are dripped into rabbits' eyes to see what effects they cause. In rabbits this can lead to swollen eyelids, irritated eyes or even blindness.
However, studies have shown that rabbits' eyes are different from those of human beings and that the tests cannot predict how human eyes will react to the substances.

2.1 Communities and identities

People have different ideas about what a community is and for many it is about belonging. Everyone needs to feel that he or she belongs.

Most people really feel they belong to the communities of people that they have something in common with, such as their age, their language, particular interests and hobbies, the job they do, or the religious beliefs they all share. Many people are part of, and feel they belong to, several communities that overlap – for example, school, friends, family and neighbours, clubs, ethnic group, church.

Wei, Michael and Grace belong to several communities:

Neighbourhood

Social network

Wei

School

Girl Guides

Michael

Online game

Football

Youth club

Chess club

Grace

Sports centre

Friends

Church

Dance club

Activity

1 Draw a diagram to show the different communities you feel you belong to.

2 Are these all with people your own age or do you share communities with people of different ages?

3 Create a class list of all the different types of communities.

Identities

Belonging to different communities and cultures is part of what gives people their sense of identity. It is different for every person, because some things are more important to them than others.

Activity

Look at the following influences on cultural identity and decide which ones are important for you.

> **Culture** means those things that we learn from our upbringing and the people around us. It includes things like our traditions, religious beliefs, the things we hold dear (values), food and clothes. All of these influence our lives and behaviour. Some of these influences we pass on to our own children.

Family

Food

Customs and traditions

Education

Job

Where you live

Language

Symbols

Clothing

Place of birth

Religion

Friends

Interests and hobbies

Sports and teams

Music

Different identities

Activity

1. Make a collage of your own different identities.
2. Pin the collages up on the wall and go round and look at everybody's collages. Discuss the different identities in the class.

- How are people different?
- What influences do people share?
- How important is your cultural identity to you?

2.2 Living together in communities

Communities do not always live happily together.

Sometimes people judge each other by things like age, ethnic group, religion, wealth or class. They don't get to know each other, so they don't trust each other.

In some areas of the country, there is a mixture of people from many different parts of the world. Some of these people were born in Britain and are British, and it is their parents or grandparents who came here years ago. When people with different customs, languages and traditions live in the same area, they often do not meet each other. They tend to mix only with people like themselves. This can lead to misunderstandings and possible conflict, as in the examples on the next page.

Activity

1 Work in pairs. Read the descriptions of the three communities on the page opposite and look carefully at the illustrations that go with them. Then look at the issues in the boxes.

   a Decide which of these issues apply to the different communities (some apply to more than one).
   b Explain their impact on each community.

2 Discuss as a pair whether there are similar problems in your community, where different groups do not mix or are uneasy together.

3 Pool your ideas in class discussion about the sorts of problems and issues that arise in mixed areas.

Newcomers

Not enough work in the area

Different religions and customs

Lack of facilities for young people

People not mixing

Type of housing

Violence and fear of crime and violence

Cost of housing

Inequalities of wealth (rich and poor)

Little Chifford is a village in a beautiful part of the countryside, near the sea. Rich people from other parts of the country have bought cottages here as second homes. They come at weekends and in the summer. They don't really mix with the locals.

Local people can't afford to buy houses in the village and they blame the second-home owners for pushing up prices. Most young people leave to work in nearby towns. Farmers in the area can't get anyone to do work in their fields and so they employ seasonal foreign workers, who often live in caravans.

The foreign workers don't mix with the locals either and the local people are not friendly. There have been some fights between the foreign workers and the local youth.

Brantborough is a borough in a large city. There are several large housing estates where many of the poorest families live. There is very little for young people who live on the estates to do, so they often meet each other outside and hang about talking, smoking and drinking.

Older people on the estate are frightened of these big groups of young people. They don't go out at night and they put bars on their doors to protect themselves. The young people get involved in vandalism and fights. Parents are worried that their children will be injured or killed. Everyone seems to be frightened – the old, the young and the parents.

Swatton is an old industrial town which used to produce cloth in large mills. At its busiest, many workers were needed and people came from abroad to work in the mills. Cheap cloth can now be imported and the industry has died. The mills have been done up and are now apartment blocks or business premises. The immigrant workers have settled, found other work and had children and grandchildren. The groups don't mix much and the town now has two different groups who live in different parts of the town, have different religions, follow different customs, eat different food, etc. There are sometimes disagreements between the groups, often because one group thinks that the others are getting better treatment from the council.

Activity

Look at this imaginary community. It has plenty of housing but no facilities. Imagine that a mixture of people are going to move in – old people, young families, single people, all of different ethnic backgrounds and with different traditions and religions.

Working in small groups, give your community a name. Then decide which **four** facilities are the most important for the community to help people get on well. Say why you have chosen these four and then suggest **one** more that is not illustrated.

Would you add places of worship? Explain your reasons.

Pub

Nursery

School

Shop

Youth club

Post office

Activity

1 **a** Look at the suggestions below and decide which of the suggestions you agree with.

    b Choose two which you consider to be the best or most important.

2 Can you think of any other solutions? Write your suggestions on sticky notes and display them on a board. Vote on the best suggestions.

Café

Town hall

Community centre

Library

Theatre

Cinema

Have a swimming pool and sports centre that local people can afford to use.

Make sure that schools take their pupils from the different ethnic groups in an area so that there is a good mix in each school.

Provide a community centre or place where people can meet and hold events and entertainments, e.g. to celebrate religious festivals.

Set up a café where drinks and food are cheap and there are facilities for parents with babies and toddlers.

Set up a youth shelter where young people can hang out without being hassled by the police.

Encourage the setting up of groups, e.g. a residents' committee on a housing estate, to work with local authority councillors to sort out problems.

Have a sports centre where there are many structured activities for young people.

Set up a committee for the area to arrange inter-cultural events where people from different groups can display their cultures.

Have a range of shops, e.g. greengrocer, baker, general store, in the local area to serve people's needs and allow people to meet and talk to each other.

2.4 Community services

Every community in the country needs certain services to be provided for the people who live in them. The rubbish needs to be collected, streets have to be kept clean, people need protecting from crime, children need to be educated. Also, the very young, the very old and people in need all require a range of different services for their health, education and safety.

Some of these services are provided by local councils, some by voluntary organisations and some by the national government. Services provided by the national government are paid for through various taxes and those provided by the local council are paid for through the local council tax, along with a grant from central government.

Activity

1 Work in pairs. Choose two of the following services and carry out a survey of local people to find out what they think of these services, scoring each from 1 to 5 (where 1 is poor and 5 is excellent).

Service	Person 1 score	Person 2 score	Person 3 score	Person 4 score	Person 5 score
Rubbish collection					
Sports centres					
Parks					
Libraries					
Recycling centres					
Day-care for elderly people					
Children's nurseries					
Youth service					
Meals for the elderly					

2 Collate your findings and discuss which services are well thought-of and which are not.

3 What improvements to the services could you suggest?

Voluntary groups and charities

Voluntary organisations sometimes get grants from local or central government, but very often rely on donations and voluntary help. They are usually registered charities.

There are thousands of people who do voluntary work every day. They do not get paid, although their expenses are usually covered. They do all kinds of work: providing advice, running clubs for young and old people, working in charity shops, helping people with shopping and household chores.

Why volunteer?

Volunteering takes many different forms. Sixteen-year-old Andrew Tindall reached the semi-final of BBC's *Young Apprentice*. His ambition is to be a doctor. Here he talks about his experience of volunteering.

'I volunteer in a retirement home every Sunday morning for two hours from 11 to 1. I chat to the residents and make sure they are comfortable and happy. I'll then go and visit the residents who can't leave their rooms and make sure they're having a good morning or alert the nurses if something is wrong. If the nurses want anything doing, I try to make their job a bit easier, for example, collecting people from their rooms in their wheelchairs and taking them to where they need to be.

At lunchtime I bring them to the dining room, where I hand out tea and lunch and help them eat, cutting up their food, chatting and generally trying to make them have a better Sunday. Normally families visit later in the day but some people don't have any family, so it's good for them to feel like someone is still there for them.

Volunteering enhances you as a person. I think everyone should do it, even if it's just an hour a week. It's something different to do, to take your mind off things and it gives you a perspective on life. Also, if you have grandparents who are ill, you'd want someone to be there to talk to them, make sure they're happy. If you're in college and want to go into medicine, this is a great way to get experience and fantastic to put on your CV. Wherever you volunteer, they will appreciate it.'

www.nhs.uk/Livewell/volunteering/Pages/Andrew-Tindall-volunteering.aspx

The Citizens Advice Bureau

Provides advice on a whole range of topics, such as benefits, debt, housing. Sometimes it directs people to where they can get more help and advice.

Groundwork

Works with young people – often those excluded, or at risk of being excluded, from school. It involves them in creative community projects which teach them skills for life and work.

Age UK

Campaigns on all issues related to older people to make sure they are well treated. Locally, it provides help and advice to older people on a wide range of issues.

Activity

1 Have you ever volunteered? If so, describe your experiences to the class.
2 If you have never volunteered, think about whether you would like to. What kind of help could you offer? What sort of organisation would you like to work in?
3 Does your school run volunteering programmes, such as vInspired? Find out more about the programmes running or discuss starting one through the school council.

2.5 Are you a good or an active citizen?

People on television or in newspapers often say that schools should turn their pupils into good citizens. The trouble is that they don't always agree about what a 'good citizen' is. In this exercise you are going to discuss what you think this phrase means and think about the difference between being a *good* citizen and being an *active* citizen.

Activity

1 Working in groups of two or three, look at all the statements below and on page 37 and decide which ones make a person a **GOOD** citizen. Add two statements of your own.

2 Choose the top five statements – the ones that are most important if a person is a good citizen.

3 Now look again at all of the statements. Which ones make a person an **ACTIVE** citizen? (Some of these might be the same as for the good citizen.) Add two statements of your own.

4 Choose the top five statements – the ones that are most important if a person is an active citizen.

5 As a whole class, discuss:
- which statements refer to being a good citizen
- which statements refer to being an active citizen
- which statements on the two lists are the same
- the difference between the two lists.

A good citizen ...   An active citizen ...

A votes in elections to choose who should run the country

C takes part in local campaigns, e.g. to oppose a new building or demand a pedestrian crossing

B never drops litter on the streets

D works for a local charity

E reports neighbours to the local council if they are noisy

F never has parties in case the noise disturbs the neighbours

G tells people off for dropping litter or letting their dogs foul the street

H obeys all laws and rules at all times

I stays out late at night having a good time with friends

Q takes part in a Neighbourhood Watch group to prevent crime

R is pleasant to people if they ask for help (e.g. giving directions)

J takes newspapers and bottles to the recycling centre

S takes books back to the library on time

T votes in elections to choose who should run the local council

K watches the neighbours very closely to make sure they are not up to mischief

U helps elderly neighbours and pops round to check they are OK

L has strong religious beliefs and worships regularly

V does not talk loudly on a mobile phone in a public place

M takes part in election campaigns by distributing leaflets for a political party

W does not put feet on the seats of buses and trains

N takes part in protests over important issues (e.g. where a road is being built through a beauty spot), even if this means breaking the law

X takes an interest in current affairs and watches the news

O does not write graffiti on walls

Y writes letters to MPs (Members of Parliament) or the local council about things that seem wrong

P reports vandals to the police

Some people say …
A 'good citizen' is someone who is easy to get on with and to live near because he/she obeys the rules, helps others and is responsible and considerate.

Some people say …
An 'active citizen' is also responsible, but wants to change things for the better. He/she is prepared to point out things that are not so good, to argue and take actions that will persuade other people that change is necessary.

2.6 Can you change anything?

As an active citizen, you can help to make your community a better place to live. You can try to influence the decisions of the local council, which is responsible for looking after your local area. What else can you do to have your say on what's going on in your neighbourhood?

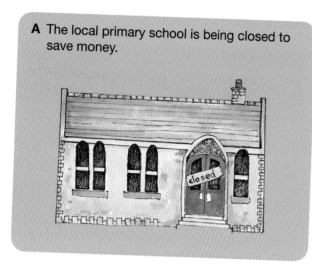

A The local primary school is being closed to save money.

What could you do?

This list shows some of the things you could do to tackle these issues.

1 Ring up the council and talk to the official responsible.
2 Write a letter of complaint to the council.
3 Go to see your local councillor. They usually hold regular 'surgeries' to listen to the complaints and problems of people in their area.
4 Draw up a petition to send to the council.
5 Write to the local newspaper, if the council does not respond.
6 Organise a local demonstration or march in connection with the issue. Invite the local newspaper along and invite local councillors to join you.
7 Take part in peaceful but disruptive behaviour, e.g. sitting down in the road, occupying houses or areas of countryside.
8 Invite your MP (Member of Parliament) to join you and/or write to your MP outlining your complaint.

Activity

1 The issues below and opposite might occur in any local area. Working in pairs, look at the 'What could you do?' list below and decide which course of action you think is appropriate in each case. Some issues are more serious than others, so you need to find an appropriate solution. Use your own ideas as well when deciding what could be done.

2 As a whole class, compare the decisions you reached and discuss why you chose each course of action rather than another.

B Some neighbours in your area are very noisy. One household down the road often plays music until three in the morning.

C A new supermarket is being built in the neighbourhood. Most local people do not want another supermarket. You want a sports centre or a skating rink.

D A building developer wants to remove a large number of ancient trees which were part of the common land near where you live. This is a site of great natural beauty with rare butterflies.

E A particular place where people cross the road has been the scene of a number of accidents. There is nowhere else to cross the road. You have begged the council to put in a proper pelican crossing, but nothing has been done. After the latest accident, in which a girl broke her leg, you agree with other local people that something has to be done.

Being an active citizen

When things in our communities are not right, it's easy to moan and complain. But perhaps something could be done. When people work together they can often help to make changes happen.

Choose an issue that concerns you in your:

- school, e.g. school dinners are small and expensive; school uniforms are unattractive

or

- neighbourhood, e.g. the local park is dirty and dangerous for young children; the youth club is often closed; the local buses are full and drivers won't let children on.

Decide what action needs to be taken to improve things and what you could do to make it happen.

You need to think about:

- what information you need
- how you can find out what other people think
- what action can be taken to improve the situation
- who can help with this (e.g. influential people).

3.1 Laws and the justice system

Rules are necessary for groups of people to get on together, as we saw at the beginning of this book. Rules become laws when they are given the backing of the government of the country. These laws are written down and enforced by the police.

When people are accused of breaking the law, they are taken to court to try to find out if they are guilty or innocent. Courts decide on the punishments for people found guilty of committing crimes. Sometimes people disagree about the way the law has been enforced and, in democratic countries, there is a right of appeal to a higher court to look again at the legal process. Crime has consequences for offenders, victims and for society at large.

How does the law affect young people?

The law should treat all adults the same. It is an important part of the legal system of the UK that the same laws apply to everyone. But the law allows young people to do different things at different ages. How much do you know about your legal rights and duties?

Activity

1   Work in pairs. At what age do you think you can do the following things (below and on page 41)? See how many you can get right. Your teacher will tell you the correct answers at the end.
2   Why are you allowed to do different things at different ages?
3   Which of these laws do you think are unfair?
4   Choose just **one** and plan an argument explaining why you would like to see the law changed to a different age. Give at least **two** reasons and explain them.

10   Fly an aeroplane

9   Buy fireworks

8   Buy alcohol

7   Leave education/training and get a full-time job

6   See a 15-certificate film

1   Be held to be criminally responsible

2   Buy a pet

3   Get a part-time job

4   Go into a pub

5   Get a custodial sentence for a crime

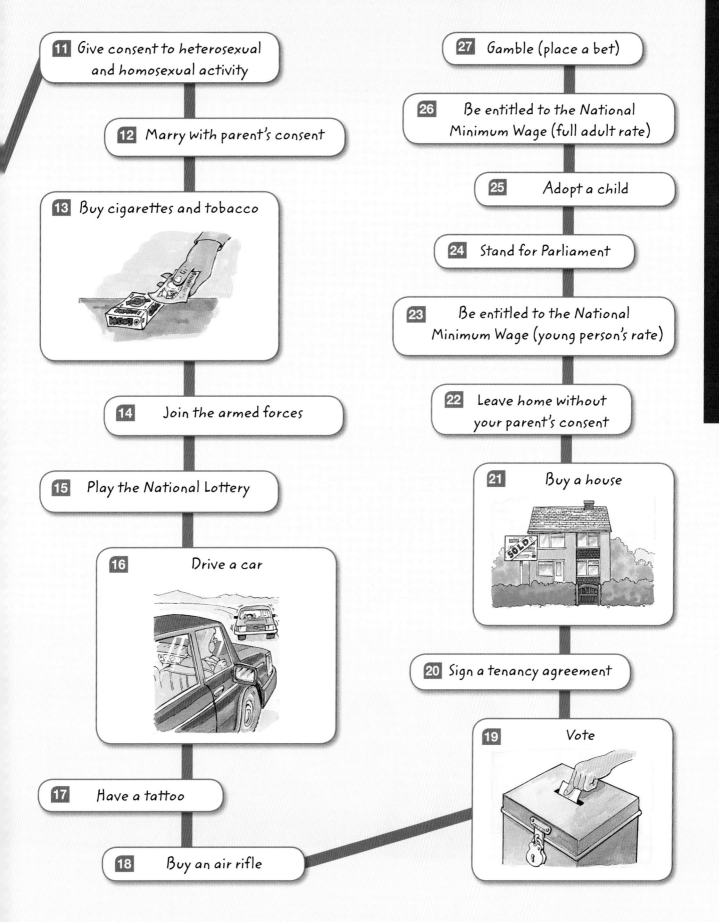

11 Give consent to heterosexual and homosexual activity

27 Gamble (place a bet)

26 Be entitled to the National Minimum Wage (full adult rate)

12 Marry with parent's consent

25 Adopt a child

24 Stand for Parliament

13 Buy cigarettes and tobacco

23 Be entitled to the National Minimum Wage (young person's rate)

14 Join the armed forces

22 Leave home without your parent's consent

15 Play the National Lottery

21 Buy a house

16 Drive a car

20 Sign a tenancy agreement

17 Have a tattoo

19 Vote

18 Buy an air rifle

3.2 Youth crime

No-one of any age is allowed to break the law. But in England, Wales and Northern Ireland, the age of criminal responsibility is 10. In Scotland it is now 12. It is thought that children younger than this do not understand that what they have done is wrong. If they commit a serious crime, social services will deal with the case. Everyone over the age of 10 is held responsible for their crimes and can be arrested, tried and, if found guilty, punished.

Some people say that children as young as 10 or 11 do not really understand the consequences of their actions. Also, some child criminals may have suffered abuse themselves, making it difficult for them to feel for others. These people would raise the age of criminal responsibility to 12.

Others say that children of 10 definitely know the difference between right and wrong, and you cannot let them get away with crime or they will go on to commit worse ones. These people would lower the age of criminal responsibility to eight (as it is in Switzerland).

What do you think?

Age of criminal responsibility in other countries

Canada	12
France	13
Germany	14
Spain	16
Belgium	18

Activity

Have a class discussion and vote on the following:

1 Keep age of criminal responsibility at 10.

2 Raise the age of criminal responsibility to 12.

3 Lower the age of criminal responsibility to 8.

Reasons why young people break the law

Feeling unloved or unhappy

History of crime in the family

Parents split up / broken home

Influenced by friends / trying to impress friends

Out of control of parents or teachers

Crime common in the neighbourhood

Excluded from school / not getting on well at school

No money for consumer goods

Drugs / alcohol

Activity

1 Do you agree with any of the reasons given for youth crime? Would you add any more reasons?

2 Look at the quotes below from young people about the reasons for their behaviour. What do they tell us about why young people commit crimes? Match the quotes to the reasons given in the boxes on the page opposite.

3 In pairs, decide on the three most important reasons for youth crime.

> **A** *It's all about who you grow up with … If you grew up in a rough area, with all people doing crime, smoking dope and whatever, doing drugs, the kids that grew up in that area they've got a bigger chance that they'll end up like that as well.*

> **B** *[I was] slung out of my house at 11 years of age, no mum to love me, no brothers, nothing… It's the love that your family has to give you that can stop [you offending], nothing else. If your mum and dad show you neglect, I guarantee you, you're going into crime.*

> **C** *On the street you're looking for a hard reputation …*

> **D** *Kids hang out in groups, some of them are criminals already, and they dare them to do a house robbery or something like that … so they end up going to do it and they get lucky and get away with it … if they think they can earn about £1,000 by doing a house or two … not a likely chance of getting caught, so why not?*

> **E** *Problems at home led me to hang around street corners. I got into drugs, I didn't have any money so I started stealing, then I got on to car theft, things like that.*

▲ These quotes are adapted from *Wasted Lives* published by the National Association for the Care and Resettlement of Offenders (NACRO).

Answers

1: 10 (in England, Wales and Northern Ireland); 2: 16; 3: 13; 4: 14; 5: 15; 6: 15; 7: 18; 8: 18; 9: 18; 10: 17 (21 for commercial pilot); 11: 16;
12: 16 (without consent in Scotland); 13: 18; 14: 16 (with parent's consent); 15: 16; 16: 17; 17: 18; 18: 18; 19: 18 (16 in Scotland);
20: 18 (16 in Scotland); 21: 18; 22: 18; 23: 18; 24: 18; 25: 21; 26: 21 (full adult rate); 27: 18.

3.3 Rights and the police

The police need powers if they are to do their job of preventing crime and arresting suspects. Many of us are likely to come into contact with the police at some time in our lives, whether as victims of crime, witnesses or suspects. It is important that we are treated properly, whatever the reason for dealings with the police. For this reason, there are laws and codes of practice which say how police officers should use their powers when carrying out their duties.

Stop and search

Some young people will experience 'stop and search' on the streets, especially in large cities.

1   The police have the power to stop and search you in the street, or in your vehicle, if they have 'reasonable suspicion' that you are carrying:
    - controlled illegal drugs
    - an offensive weapon
    - stolen goods
    - tools for a burglary or theft
    - alcohol to a sports fixture
    - alcohol or tobacco if you are under-age.

2   'Reasonable suspicion' must be based on your behaviour and not on the kind of person you are (race, age, nationality, and so on), or how you are dressed. However, if they think you are wearing something to try to hide your identity and that a violent crime might be committed, they can ask you to remove it.

3   Before the search, the police officer should give:
    - proof that he or she is a police officer, by showing a warrant card
    - information on police powers to stop and search and the individual's rights in these circumstances
    - his or her name and police station
    - the grounds for the search
    - how to get hold of a record of the search.

4   The police can ask you to remove outer clothing for a search in the street, but would need to take you to a more private place, such as a police van, if other clothing or shoes are removed. You must be searched by someone of the same gender.

5   You can only be forced to go to a police station if you are arrested. You could be arrested if you refuse to co-operate with the police and refuse to give your name and address.

Arrest

1 You should be told why you have been arrested and the police should caution you, as follows:

'You do not have to say anything. But it may harm your defence if you do not mention when questioned something which you later rely on in court. Anything you do say may be given in evidence.'

2 Someone should be told of your arrest and you should be able to see a solicitor, although you do not necessarily have the right to a phone call.

3 You can be held at the police station for 24 hours without charge, but this can be 36 hours for some serious offences. In an extreme case, such as allegations of terrorism, the police can apply to a magistrate to keep someone for up to 72 hours.

Interview and charge

1 If you are under 17, an 'appropriate adult' should be present while you are interviewed. This could be a family member, a solicitor or a teacher, for example.

2 The interview will be tape-recorded.

3 After the interview the police may:
- charge you with an offence
- remand you in custody
- release you on police bail
- release you after a formal caution
- release you without charge.

4 If you are charged, the custody officer will read out the charges against you and ask if you have anything to say. You will receive a copy of the charges and a date of the court appearance.

5 You may be finger-printed and photographed. If you refuse to have your fingerprints taken, the police can apply to a magistrate to make you agree.

Activity

1 Work in pairs. Complete a table like the one below.

	Summary of police powers	Summary of rights of the suspect
Stop and search		
Arrest		
Interview and charge		

2 In your pairs, decide which of the rights of the suspect is the most important. Explain why.

What advice would you give?

1 Ali, Jordan, Suzy and Donna are friends of yours. Each of them has come up against the police in the last few weeks. They don't know their rights and need your help. Read each situation below and on page 47 and answer the questions that relate to them.

Suzy had been shopping for clothes in town with Donna. As she left the shop, a security guard and a male police officer approached the two girls. The security guard said that he believed that Suzy had stolen some clothing. The police officer asked her to open her shopping, but Suzy refused. The police officer insisted and said that if she wouldn't let him, he'd have to arrest her and take her to the police station. So Suzy agreed, but when she opened her bags, there was no stolen clothing in there.

Did the police officer have the legal right to search Suzy's bag?

When Suzy's bags were found to be empty, the security guard turned to Donna. He said that she had probably stuffed the stolen clothes up inside her jacket. He asked the police officer to search her then and there, before the two girls tried to run off. The police officer grabbed Donna and took off her jacket, though Donna tried to stop him. There were no stolen goods under the jacket.

Did the police officer have the right to search Donna?

Jordan and Ali were hanging about with some friends on the estate where they live. A fight started between two of the other boys and it got really nasty as one of the boys pulled a knife. A neighbour called the police and all the boys were arrested and taken to the police station. The knife had been dropped on the ground, so the police wanted to take everyone's fingerprints to see who had been holding it. Jordan and Ali allowed their fingerprints to be taken, but were not sure that they had to.

Did the police have the legal right to take Jordan's and Ali's fingerprints?

The police interviewed each of the boys separately. Jordan, who is 16, wanted his mum to come to the police station, but she had her mobile turned off and the police couldn't contact her. They decided to interview him on his own because they had interviewed all of the others with their parents and wanted to clear the matter up.

Did the police have the legal right to interview Jordan?

Activity

1 Work in threes. One of you should take on the role of the suspect of a crime, one an arresting officer and one an observer. Role-play a street arrest for a suspected robbery. Both the police officer and the suspect should act responsibly. If either is unreasonable, it could affect their future position in court.

   The observer should note down any mistakes made by the suspect and by the police officer and should report what has been noted at the end of the role play.

2 Do you think the police have sufficient powers to do their job properly? Should they have more powers or fewer powers?

3.4 What happens to young offenders?

The UK youth justice system uses three main ideas when dealing with offenders:
1 They should **take responsibility** for what they have done.
2 They should **make amends** to the victims of the crime or to the community.
3 They should be **given help** to get back on the right track and stop offending.

How the youth justice system works for young people aged 10–17

Who decides	What you get
Police The police decide whether to give an informal warning, a reprimand or a final warning. 	**An informal warning** If a young person commits a first minor offence, they might get an informal warning or 'telling off'. *Or* **A reprimand (an official 'telling off')** This is given at the police station with an appropriate adult present if the young person admits their guilt. This goes on the young person's criminal record. *Or* **A final warning** If the offence is more serious, or the young person has been in trouble before, they will be given a final warning. This means they will be referred to a Youth Offending Team. The team decides what action needs to be taken to stop the young person from offending again.
Youth Offending Team (YOT) The YOT is made up of members of the police and social services, and education, probation and health agencies in a local area. 	
Youth Court This is a special court for young people, heard by magistrates. 	**Sent to Youth Court** If the offence is serious, or it is a second or third offence, the person will be charged and sent straight to a Youth Court for trial. The magistrates decide whether the young person is guilty, and if so, what the punishment should be. If the offender is under 10, there will be no trial, but the Youth Court will be asked to make a Child Safety Order.

What do you think should happen to each of the offenders described in the coloured boxes? Should they:

- get a reprimand?
- receive a final warning and be referred to the YOT?
- be sent to the Youth Court?

Think about how old each offender is, what they have done and how serious the offence is.

Asif is 11 years old and has been getting into trouble a lot at school. He was seen on camera damaging cars in the school car park. This is not his first case of vandalism. He is well known on his estate for breaking windows and getting into fights.

Greta is 14 and has been found in possession of drugs – mostly pills. The police suspect that she has been supplying them to other young people. Greta has been excluded from school for persistent bad behaviour and rudeness to teachers.

Daryl is 16 and has stolen an elderly woman's handbag in the street, pushing her to the ground. He already has a final warning from the police for theft. His parents are not able to control Daryl and say he has got in with a bad lot of friends. He has not responded to the programme of the Youth Offending Team in connection with his final warning.

Marcie is 16 and the mother of a baby boy aged 6 months. She was caught shoplifting from a clothes store. It is her first offence. She says she has no money to buy clothes and wanted something for a party. She is worried that the baby will be put into care if she is taken into custody.

Youth Offending Team

If a young person gets a final warning, they are referred to a Youth Offending Team (YOT) which might include social workers, youth workers and probation officers. They will draw up a programme which aims to change the young person's behaviour; it is not meant to be a punishment. The programme will cover:

- reasons why the young person got into trouble
- help for parents to control the young person better
- counselling for the young person
- community activities
- an apology to the victim and repair of any damage
- improvement to school work and attendance.

Here is a possible programme for a young person who has been in trouble for fighting at school and has been caught spraying graffiti:

Programme

- Attend three sessions with a YOT worker, looking at the consequences of their actions.
- Attend group sessions on anger management.
- Assist a local community group that is preparing a mural in a local youth club.

Activity

Can you suggest a programme for Daryl, Asif, Greta or Marcie?

3.5 The Youth Court

If young people commit a serious offence or if they reoffend after a final warning, the case goes to a Youth Court. The Youth Court is a type of magistrates' court specially designed for young people under the age of 18. It is less formal than adult courts; the magistrates are specially trained and they have a different range of sentences they can pass. The cases are held in private: members of the public are not allowed in. The parents of the young person are generally expected to attend.

Activity

1 Match each label (A to H) to the appropriate numbered person in the court.

2 The class could undertake a roleplay of the magistrates' court using the cases and sentences on pages 52–53.

A Witness

A police officer might give details of the offence or another person might say what happened. Witnesses only attend if the young person says he or she is not guilty.

B Usher

The usher calls in the witnesses.

C Magistrates

Two or three magistrates sit behind a big desk (the bench). They are men and women chosen from the community (not lawyers) who decide whether the young person has committed the offence and how they are going to be dealt with. Most magistrates are not paid. One of the magistrates (usually the one in the middle) is the chairperson and speaks for them all.

D Youth Offending Team

The Youth Offending Team consists of local professionals, such as social workers, probation officers and the police, who may have come across the young person before. Some of the team might attend court proceedings and sit at the back of the court.

E Young person, parents and solicitor

The young person who is charged with the offence (the defendant) sits in the middle of the court in front of the bench. The parents sit on one side and a solicitor usually sits on the other. The solicitor, a trained lawyer, is there to protect the legal rights of the young person.

F Justice's clerk

The clerk sits at the side or in front of the magistrates. The clerk is a trained lawyer and advises the magistrates on the law. The clerk reads out the charge (the offence the young person is said to have committed) and asks whether he/she pleads guilty or not. The clerk has no say in deciding whether the young person is guilty and does not decide what should happen to them, although he/she may tell the magistrates what alternatives are open to them.

G Prosecutor

The prosecutor is a solicitor whose job is to set out the case against the young person for the police. The prosecutor provides the evidence to show that the person committed the offence.

H Victim

Victims may come to court if they wish, and may be involved before the magistrates decide on any sentence.

Activity

How good do you think you would be at deciding what sentence an offender should receive? Work in groups of three magistrates. Discuss each case below, decide what you are trying to achieve (look at the chart on page 53), then decide on the sentence and give your reasons for it. Write down your sentence and why you chose it.

The cases

A Sarah, 15 years old, has been found guilty of stealing £40 from an old lady who lives on her estate. She has helped the old lady at times, doing small jobs for her, but this time she took the money from her purse.

B Jasmina, 17, has been convicted for selling drugs, mainly cannabis and ecstasy. She deals drugs to fund her own drug habit. She has also been arrested before for petty theft. She is living in a flat with friends. She was brought up in a children's home.

C Billy has been found guilty of robbery with assault. He stole goods and money from a small store. With two accomplices, he also beat and kicked the storekeeper who tried to stop him. Billy has a violent history of being involved in fights in the local area. His father violently abused him when he was a child.

D Kenneth has been part of a gang stopping school students on the way home from school and taking their money and mobile phones. They never hurt anybody because the victims were too frightened to do anything, but they did threaten violence.

E Marek has been convicted of taking a vehicle and driving it away with a group of friends. He had been drinking alcohol and the vehicle crashed into the pavement, injuring an old man who is still in hospital with a broken leg.

F Rosie has been found guilty of shoplifting. It is her second appearance in court for this offence, but she has been stopped by security staff before and not prosecuted. She usually steals clothes or make-up. She has a job in a café, but does not earn much money.

To help offenders be better citizens and stop offending

To give criminals what they deserve – punishment!

To deter others from offending

What is the purpose of sentencing?

To make victims feel they have received justice

To make the community a safer place

Sentences

You can give a combination of orders. This means you might award a compensation order, a reparation order and a supervision order for a particular offender.

- **A fine**
- **Compensation order**
  Money paid to victim, usually up to £1,000.
- **Reparation order**
  This means putting things right. It could involve repairing damage, writing an apology or meeting the victim face-to-face to talk about the crime.

Action plan order

This can require offenders to:

- join anger management classes or drug/alcohol misuse programmes
- present themselves at particular times at specified places
- go to an attendance centre for a certain number of hours
- stay away from specified places, e.g. shopping centres
- carry out work of benefit to the community, e.g. clean a local canal.

Custodial order

Offenders over 15 can be sent to a young offenders' institution for a period of time. Alternatively (especially for younger offenders), half the sentence is spent in a local authority secure unit or training centre and half under supervision in the community.

Attendance order

Offenders have to report to a centre, usually run by the police, for two hours twice a month for between 12 and 36 hours in total.

Curfew order

This means the offender has to stay home for a specified part of the day.

Supervision order

The offender is supervised by a social worker, probation officer or another member of a Youth Offending Team for between three months and three years.

Parenting order

Parents are told by the court to have greater control over their child. The parents may have to attend parenting classes to learn how to do this. A fine of £1,000 is made if the parents do not agree to this.

Activity

Take each case in turn and discuss the sentences given by different groups of pupils. Use these questions to help you:

- What sentence was given?
- Did the magistrate give good reasons for their sentence?

- What did the sentence seek to achieve for the offender?
- Did the sentence consider the victims?
- At the end of each case, agree in the class what the fairest sentence is.
- How difficult was it to reach a sentence that was fair?

3.7 Inside a young offenders' institution

If a young offender is over the age of 15, he or she can be sentenced to custody in a young offenders' institution (YOI). What is it like inside? What experiences do the young people have? Does it help them or does it turn them into hardened criminals?

The views below and on page 55 are compiled from interviews with several young people (not shown in these photos) who have spent quite a lot of time in YOIs. Most of them have long records of offending, stretching back to the ages of 12 and 13. What they have in common now is the desire not to spend any more time in prison.

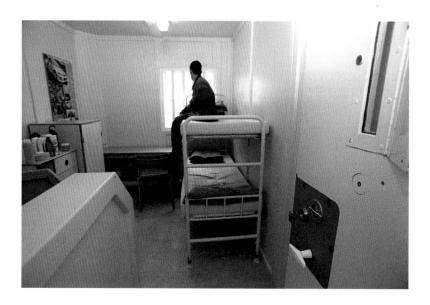

What are YOIs like inside?

'The YOIs in old prisons can be dirty, paint peeling off walls and the like. Others are modern or have been done up and are all right. The cells are small and usually you share. Apart from a double bunk bed, you have a table, a wash basin and metal chairs fixed to the wall – not much else. You can have a radio and a CD player. But whatever the cells are like, it does your head in to be stuck in them for so long each day. The boredom is a real killer.'

What's the daily routine like?

'It varies with the institution. In some of them you're banged up in your cell for over 18 hours a day and you get very little exercise and not much association time – that's mixing with other inmates. In other places you're banged up for less time, 15 to 16 hours. You get more leisure time, say 2 hours' association time every evening, 1 hour's exercise, 2 hours' education, and so on. But you often spend a lot of time in your cell. In some places you can get jobs and earn some money (not much) gardening, in the kitchens or as a landing cleaner. You can spend that on your canteen. Once a week you are given your money, about £2.50, and you can spend it on tobacco, sweets, that kind of thing.'

What are the worst things about being inside?

'You don't know what's going on outside. Say you've got trouble with your family. It only takes one person to say something and, together with everything else that's in your head, it makes you feel bad and frustrated because you can't do anything. Also with girlfriends there's so much stress; you think she's out clubbing; she's seeing someone; you feel paranoid because you don't know what's going on – it drives you mad … And there's never enough food! You're always hungry … And the boredom!

There's a lot of violence and bullying. In prison you've got nothing, so things mean something. I've seen a fight over a packet of biscuits. Whenever somebody has something, others think they should have a share. And there'll always be someone who takes it all to show how hard they are. If you go round the cells in a prison, there will always be people who can't fight to save their lives. But they can survive in jail by bartering: swap something; sell something; do things for people. You can feel very threatened.

Once I never came out of my cell much for two weeks because five lads were waiting to get me. I sat in my cell with a chair leg ready to have a go. Eventually, I got myself put into solitary and then got shipped out to another YOI.'

Do YOIs help you to change?

'In some ways they make things worse because you build up a network of new contacts with criminals, people who say "See me when you get out", and they introduce you to their friends and get you drugs, etc. Also you feel so angry and frustrated that when you do get out you're likely to go and get yourself into trouble.

The education – basic maths and English, cooking, computers – is quite useful. But the officers, apart from a few, aren't interested much. You can't blame them, they're just doing a job, and most of the inmates don't want help, they just want to do their time and get out and go back to their old life. In three and a half years only one officer, a female officer, has been really helpful and tried to encourage me to change when I leave prison. You need much more advice about how to get jobs and more help to find places to live and start again in a new place. Because if you go back to where you were, you just slip into your old ways.'

Activity

1 From these accounts, what do you think is the worst thing about being inside a YOI?

2 Do you think changes should be made to YOIs or not?

3 Would changes to the system help young offenders to change their behaviour?

4 Hold a class discussion on whether imprisoning young people works.

3.8 Adult courts

There are two kinds of adult courts: civil or criminal.

Civil courts deal with disagreements that people have about property, divorce, child custody, compensation claims, etc. Civil law involves situations where someone feels that damage has been done to them and so brings a case against another person or organisation. The person bringing the case is called a 'plaintiff'. Examples of cases might be claims against someone who caused an accident, failed in a professional duty or wrote something that damaged someone else's reputation.

Most civil cases are heard in a county court, but more serious and complicated cases go to a high court. Some civil cases are heard in front of a jury. People can appeal decisions in civil law, and the highest court in the land is the Supreme Court, which will make decisions on important points of civil law.

Criminal courts deal with people who have been accused of breaking a law and who face some kind of punishment, if found guilty. In our country, criminal cases are usually heard first in a magistrates' court. If the case is not serious, the magistrates will come to a decision about guilt and sentence (which will be limited according to the offence).

More serious offences are heard in crown courts, where a judge is in charge, but guilt is decided by a jury. Very serious offences (e.g. murder, armed robbery, rape or large frauds) are heard in a high court, but also in front of a jury.

Activity

Decide which of these cases would be heard in a civil court and which in a criminal court.

1 A couple who are getting divorced cannot agree about who should have custody of the children.

3 A newspaper publishes something about a particular person, which that person says is a lie.

DAILY NEWS EXCLUSIVE
TOP CELEBRITY NAMED IN CHILD ABUSE SCANDAL

2 A young man breaks into a house and steals a lot of jewellery.

4 A drunk driver has an accident and injures a pedestrian.

Juries in criminal courts

A jury in England and Wales is made up of 12 people from all walks of life. Anybody between 18 and 70 years of age can be called for jury service if they appear on the electoral roll (i.e. they can vote in elections). Jury service is compulsory unless you have a very good reason for not attending. You are paid a small amount to make up for loss of earnings.

Some countries do not have juries and judges make the decisions about guilt or innocence. People disagree about the value of juries, although they go back a long way in the history of this country. There have been examples of juries being intimidated, and sometimes of jurors breaking the rules by looking up a case on the internet or falling asleep during a case. But many people think that 12 ordinary people are best suited to deciding whether or not someone is guilty. They think that trial by jury is an important part of our democracy, although some politicians have argued that juries are too expensive and time-consuming.

Activity

Work in pairs and look at the arguments listed below. Discuss the arguments and decide whether you are in favour of juries or not. Can you think of any more arguments that support your view of juries?

Arguments in favour of juries

1 Having a jury of ordinary people makes sure that trials are not controlled by rich and powerful people.

2 A jury is likely to be made up of a mix of people from different backgrounds – social class, religions and ethnicity.

3 Ordinary people are more able to understand the situation faced by the defendant because they or their families may have faced similar circumstances.

4 Judges can be out of touch because they live a more privileged life and tend not to meet ordinary people.

Arguments against juries

1 Trial by jury is very expensive.

2 Jurors can be bribed, threatened or intimidated by friends of the accused.

3 Trial by jury takes a long time because the jury has to be given notice and also everything has to be carefully explained, whereas a judge could hear a case very quickly.

4 Jurors may have fixed opinions about different types of people and these stereotypes may influence their views.

3.9 Punishment for adult criminals

Punishment of adult criminals has a number of purposes.

The rest of society, and especially the victims of the crime, need to know that the offender did not 'get away with it', and that they are paying the price.

B Deterrence

A Punishment of offenders

C Reform and rehabilitation of offenders

Punishment is meant to deter the offender from committing future crimes and also prevent others from committing crime, for fear of the same punishment.

If offenders are 'shown the error of their ways' and given education or training, they might get back on their feet and stop offending in future.

D Protection of the public

E Making good to those affected by the crime

Some punishments put the offenders under supervision or even lock them away in order to protect others from their dangerous behaviour.

Sometimes people want to feel that the offender is sorry for the crime and is trying to make amends.

Activity

1 Statements A to E give different reasons for sending an offender to prison. Give each statement a mark from 1 to 5 (1 = strongly disagree; 5 = strongly agree) to show how much you agree with each view.

2 Compare the marks you have given with others in the class and discuss what you think should be the main purposes of punishment. Do you think it should be more about harsh treatment and deterrence or more about reform and rehabilitation?

Every crime, however small, has consequences. Most crimes have victims who suffer loss or injury, sometimes affecting them for the rest of their lives. But there are also consequences for all of us in different ways:

- fear of crime, which can deeply affect people's lives
- the cost in money and time – health costs, emergency services
- insurance costs for theft and damage.

Restorative justice

There is a recent trend towards 'mediation'. This means that if both the offender and the victim agree, they can meet and talk about what happened and how they both feel about it. Victims sometimes find that they need to talk about the pain, damage or loss that the crime caused. It provides them with the opportunity to get answers to their questions, to gain an understanding as to why the offence happened and help them to move on with their lives. The offender is often shocked to hear how their victim has suffered and feels very sorry.

This is what one offender said about 'restorative justice' (RJ):

'For me RJ was one of the hardest things I had ever done. In the past a victim was just a piece of paper in the form of a statement and it was easy for me to justify my actions to a faceless A4 piece of paper. The day I actually sat in the same room as the persons I had harmed/burgled was probably the most profound day in my life; it seemed like the victims were saying "you caused us a lot of pain, so, now you are here we would like to share the pain with you".

After spending 18+ years of my life in prisons and other similar establishments, and a lifetime of hurting people, I found myself hearing exactly how I had left these people feeling.

At court it was not anything to do with the victim, it was all about breaking the rules and being punished! RJ was different, I heard first-hand how much pain I had caused, not the physical pain, the emotional, mental and spiritual pain I had inflicted.

To try and tell you what happened in words during that meeting is impossible really, it was more of "how it left me feeling", it was as if for the first time I really and truly understood, and what's more, for the first time in my life really cared about the people I had hurt.'

Activity

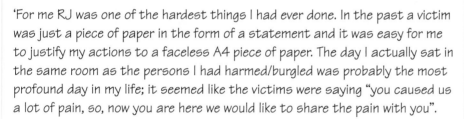

1 What are the consequences for the people shown in the illustration above? How do you think they will be affected in the future?
2 Discuss the idea of restorative justice. What are the advantages and possible disadvantages of this form of mediation?
3 Does this change your views about the purpose of punishment?

4.1 Why do we use money?

Before money, people had to barter with each other. This means they had to exchange goods with one another.

You can see the problems this might cause. You may want to exchange something with someone but they might not want to exchange something with you. Also it is difficult to work out what something is worth compared with other goods, e.g. how many apples is a chicken worth?

To make exchange easier, people used money. From early on they used coins – pieces of precious metal – for money.

A medium of exchange

Money acts as a medium of exchange. You sell some goods or get money in wages and then you can spend it on a variety of things that you need. It does not have to be coins or precious metal. People have used some strange things for money such as beads, cowrie shells, grain, playing cards and cigarettes. As long as people are confident they will be able to exchange the money for other things, it works. We now use paper money which has no real value at all. We trust that we are going to get certain goods or services for it. The money used in a country is called its currency, e.g. the British pound, the Euro or the American dollar.

Two other functions of money

A store of wealth

You can keep your money safe and store it to use in the future.

A measure of value

We can decide what something is worth by giving it a value in money, e.g. a smartphone costs £300. This helps when we are buying or selling goods and services, not just in this country but also around the world.

A money problem

The value of money can change over time. It can lose its value: this is called 'inflation'. It often occurs when there are too few goods and people are prepared to pay more and more money for them. In the great inflation of 1923 in Germany, paper money lost its value so that you needed huge amounts of it just to buy a loaf of bread. A little bit of inflation is not a problem but it's a disaster if money loses its value quickly.

▲ Children playing with money in Germany in 1923

▲ In Bristol, you can use Bristol pounds to pay for things in shops and businesses. You can still buy things with ordinary pounds and pence but using Bristol currency helps support the businesses there and may keep some people in jobs.

Swapping

Bartering is not dead. Towns and villages all over the UK are swapping food. People with surplus home-made or home-grown food post a message on a website, like Facebook, and wait for someone to respond who has something to swap for their produce. Some towns and villages hold monthly events where people can trade with each other. It's a good way of saving money, reduces waste and brings communities together, breaking down barriers of age and culture. People get to know each other.

It's not just food. A growing number of websites help people to exchange gadgets, toys, games, books, baby and toddler items. On one website you can earn virtual currency, called 'swapits', for each item you trade.

Activity

Design your own school currency. What could it be used for and how would you earn it? What would happen if it was easy to copy so that everyone quickly became school currency millionaires?

Activity

1   Draw a diagram to show the main functions of money in society.
2   Why are trust and confidence essential to the usefulness of money?
3   a   Draw two simple cartoons to show the disadvantages of bartering goods.
    b   Explain how bartering can still be good for people and communities today.
4   Imagine there was high inflation in the UK, so that money was worth less and less each day. What would be the impact on:
    a   the way people spend money on and their attitude to food and other goods?
    b   people who had saved lots of money in a bank?
    c   people in debt owing lots of money to the bank?

4.2 What do you do with your money?

Our attitudes towards money are crucial to how we manage it, especially how much risk we are prepared to take with it. Usually if we have a sum of money, our main choices are to:

Spend it

This is enjoyable but once it's gone, it's gone; although we may have something to show for it.

Put it away

Just keep it somewhere safe for future spending.

Save it

Put it into a savings account where it earns interest (see page 73). This means that the amount of money grows. How much it grows depends on the interest rate.

Invest it

This means you buy shares in businesses with the hope that you can earn a lot of profit on your investment. But you can lose money on shares as well as gain it.

Activity

1 What would you do if you were given £50?

Would you:

a spend it?   d lend it?
b save it?   e invest it to make more money?
c give it away?

Or would it be a combination, e.g. spend some, give some away, etc.?

2 Compare your answers with others in the class and their reasons. Then think about the following:

a Are there right and wrong choices about what to do with it?

b What does this tell us about:

- our attitudes to money, e.g. careful with money, prepared to risk it to get more, selfish about it?

- what we value in our lives, e.g. things, other people?

- how money can make us feel, e.g. happy, sad, worried?

Where do you keep your money?

Most people use banks or building societies as a convenient place to keep their money safe. The money is kept in an account which can be used to manage money day to day. Most organisations pay wages or benefits into a bank account. If you don't have one, it can be more difficult to manage your financial affairs, e.g. get money paid to you or take out loans. Many people cannot get bank accounts for various reasons – e.g. previous bad debts, poor employment record – and it makes their lives much harder.

Current account

The most common account in a bank or building society is the current account. You pay in (deposit) money and you take out (withdraw) money when you need it. Every so often you receive a 'statement' which shows how much you have paid in and how much you have taken out. This is useful because your withdrawals are itemised. You can see exactly when you took money out or paid for things.

A basic bank account lets you take money out and put money in but does not have the other features of a current account, e.g. an overdraft. You can have a cash card but you can only take out what is in the account.

Cash card
This allows you to take out a cash sum (e.g. up to £250) from a bank ATM 'hole in the wall' machine. You can only take out money that is in the account. Some young people are only allowed cash cards with a basic bank account.

Direct debits
This is a regular payment to a company/business from which you are buying something, e.g. a monthly payment to an energy company for electricity. The company requests the payment from the bank. There are rules attached to direct debits to prevent money being taken out of your account without you knowing.

Cheques
You can write out a cheque to somebody or a company and give/send it to them. This tells your bank to give them a certain amount of money.

What does a current account provide?

Standing order
A regular fixed payment to somebody, e.g. £40 every three months for your TV licence.

Overdrafts
Most accounts will let you have an 'overdraft' – a sum of money you can use when you don't have any left in your account (see page 66).

Debit card
This allows you to take out cash from an ATM but also to pay for goods and services in shops and online. The money you take out and items you buy will be shown on your bank statement.

Activity

1 Design a current account for a 15–16-year-old school pupil. What features (e.g. cards, cash limits, etc.) should it have to help the teenager manage their finances without letting them get into financial trouble?

2 Do you think the government should make sure that everyone can get a basic bank account?
   a Discuss the arguments for and against this. Think about why it is so crucial to have a current account to be able to function in society.
   b Then hold a class vote to answer the question.

4.3 What's the best way to pay for things?

In the past most people paid for things in cash. You simply handed over the money. In today's world there are many different ways to pay for things. People still use cash but increasingly they use 'plastic' – credit or debit cards. All these methods have advantages and disadvantages. Let's look at the three most common methods of payment used in everyday life. You can see some other ways people pay in the box on the right.

Other ways of paying

- Mobile phones – some can be tapped on a reader to make a payment.
- Cheques – you write a cheque and give it or send it to the person/organisation you are paying.
- PayPal – used to buy things online through websites such as eBay.
- Digital money, like Bitcoin, created for the internet.

Cash

Debit card

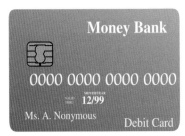

Money is taken directly from your bank account. It you have enough money in the account, this is a simple and easy method of payment. If you don't, the account will become 'overdrawn' and the bank will make you pay charges.

Credit card

This allows you to buy things now and pay for them later. All these items go on to a monthly statement. If you don't pay all the money owed each month, you get charged interest on any money outstanding. Most credit cards also provide some protection for the things you buy. For example, they may help you get your money back if goods are faulty or if a holiday company, from which you have bought a holiday, goes bust.

Activity

1 Draw up a table with three headings: Cash, Debit card, and Credit card. Decide which of the advantages and disadvantages listed goes under each heading (some go under more than one heading). Mark each statement with an 'A' if it is an advantage and a 'D' if it is a disadvantage.

Cash	Debit card	Credit card
It is a simple way of buying things: you hand it over and get change. **A**		

Advantages and disadvantages

It is a simple way of buying things: you hand it over and get change.

Some people don't realise how much they are spending because they don't keep track of their purchases.

There is no interest to pay because the payment comes straight from your bank account.

People can run up debts of thousands of pounds using several cards.

Interest payments can mount up very quickly if you don't pay it off at the end of each month.

You can end up with a very large amount to pay off if you are not careful.

It is not a good idea to carry a large amount of cash around as it can be lost or stolen.

If you become 'overdrawn' every month, the bank charges you for going overdrawn, e.g. £20, and charges interest on the amount overdrawn.

It makes it easier to buy things online or by telephone.

If criminals get hold of your card details, or clone your card, they can take all the money out of your bank account.

Many companies charge fees (e.g. £5) for using a credit card and some charge you for using a debit card when you buy things.

You can use this to spread the payment for a large item over several months.

You get some protection for purchases if the goods are faulty or you are cheated.

Activity

1 Look at the list of 'Goods and services' on the right. Which method of payment do you think would be the best to use in each case? Explain why.

2 Should the government step in to control the use of credit cards and fees?

Goods and services
- A bag of crisps and a bar of chocolate.
- A holiday in a foreign country including flights and hotel (fees charged for credit card).
- A smartphone (£250) or tablet (£380) bought online (fees charged for credit card and debit card).
- Tickets for a music festival at £85 each.
- A week's groceries from a supermarket costing £75.
- Three books from a bookshop.
- Getting clothes cleaned at a dry cleaners.
- A sofa costing £600.

4.4 Borrowing money

We all need to borrow money at times. But today in Britain millions of people are struggling to cope with serious debt. Many get into trouble because they are not aware of how much they are borrowing or don't realise how much it is costing them to borrow. They just ignore the debt until it overwhelms them.

Ways of borrowing

Credit cards

You can use a credit card to buy things and pay for them later. The interest rate on a credit card is usually between 15% and 25% over a year. But the credit card company calculates this and adds it on every month, e.g. if the interest rate is 24% they will charge 2% per month. Borrowing by credit card can be very convenient and useful if you are borrowing for short time periods but it can get out of hand if you don't control it.

Loans

Loans allow you to borrow larger sums of money and pay them back over a fixed period, e.g. five years. Usually you make a monthly payment. You have to balance what you can afford to pay each month with the overall cost of the loan. The longer you take to pay it off, the more interest you pay. Look at the example on the right.

Paying back a loan for £3000 at an interest rate of 15%

Loan	Period of loan	Monthly repayments (£)	Number of months	Total amount at end of loan (£)	Total interest (£)
£3000	1 year	270	12	3,234	234
£3000	3 years	103	36	3,695	695
£3000	5 years	70	60	4,194	1,194

Overdraft

This is when you withdraw more money from your bank/building society account than you have put in it. Most banks will allow you to have an overdraft for a fixed amount, e.g. £200, if you arrange this with them, but they will charge a high interest rate, e.g. over 20%. If you go overdrawn without telling them, they will not only charge you high interest but also make you pay a penalty charge. This can get very expensive indeed.

Hire purchase (HP)

Hire purchase is a different type of borrowing because you don't own the goods until you have paid for them in full. Under HP, you hire the goods and then pay an agreed amount by instalments. If you fall behind with the payments, the lender may be able to repossess (take back) the goods. Interest is paid and, while you can get good deals, you can end up paying a lot extra for the goods.

Interest

When you borrow money, you have to pay it back with some extra money. This extra money is called **interest**. It is the cost of borrowing the money. So, if you borrow £100 a year at 10% interest, you have to pay back £110 at the end of the year: the original £100 you borrowed + £10 of interest. If you save money, you can get interest on it in the same way (see page 73).

The 'interest rate' is crucial to look at when you borrow money. It is usually calculated over a year. If the interest rate is 1% you will pay an extra £1 for every £100 you borrow; if it is 25%, you will pay an extra £25 for every £100 you borrow.

Tips

When you borrow money:

- check the interest rate
- look at the overall cost (not just low monthly payments)
- read the conditions carefully
- shop around for the best deals
- look at money advice websites for information and warnings.

Activity

Look at these situations and decide what advice you would give the person involved about the things they should consider before making a decision.

A Jo is looking at an expensive camera costing £350. She could use her credit card and probably pay it off in four months. But she has seen a hire purchase deal which suggests she could pay only £20 a month over two years.

What advice would you give Jo?

B Asif wants to buy a second-hand motor-cycle that costs £2,000. He could take out a loan at 10% over three years making regular payments or he could use his credit card and probably pay off the debt in a year. The interest rate on his credit card is 15%.

What advice would you give Asif?

C Jessica wants some new clothes for a wedding. The outfit she wants costs £250. She does not have that much in her bank account but would only go £50 overdrawn. She could use her credit card but she has almost used up her limit of £1,500.

What advice would you give Jessica?

Need some money quickly?

Many people struggle to pay all their bills at the end of a month. It's easy to be in a position where you need some extra money quickly. Maybe your working hours have been cut down or you need to pay to fix an emergency like a leaking roof. How do you get the money you need, especially if you don't have access to credit cards or a bank loan?

Payday lenders

Many people turn to payday lenders who offer short-term or emergency loans at very high rates of interest. The loans are designed to be taken out for a short period and quickly repaid. You might take out a loan for £500 for a month and be asked to pay back £650, so, for one month you will have paid £150 in interest and fees. That's expensive.

If you pay it back on time, it has cost you a lot of money but it's not a disaster. If you don't, then the whole sum plus the interest is 'rolled over' for another month. You do not have to be an expert in maths to realise that you are paying back a lot of money for your original loan at interest rates of between 1000% and 4000%. Some people take out several payday loans and start to find themselves deeply in debt and in trouble. Look at the stories below.

▲ Payday lenders offer quick fixes.

Joan took out four payday loans of £300 but could not pay them back. The loans were rolled over and soon she owed over £4,000. She started working 60–70 hours a week to cope with the payments. In time, she could not pay her bills or the rent. She was harassed by constant telephone calls from the lender to pay up and threatened with losing her home.

Tom took out a £90 loan to pay for a train ticket to see his girlfriend. He was not able to pay it back and had to take out more loans. Eventually he owed £3,500 to four payday lenders.

There's something worse – loan sharks!

Payday lenders have to have a licence to operate. Loan sharks don't; they are acting illegally. They are people in the neighbourhood who lend money at very high rates of interest. If you don't pay it back on time, they may threaten you and your family and even hurt you. The Illegal Money Lending Team can provide support for people trapped by loan sharks.

Are credit unions the answer?

A credit union is like a bank but it is owned and run by its members. It is a group of people who save together and lend money to each other. There are a growing number of credit unions in the UK. They can be set up by people who live in a particular area or work together, or by people belonging to a church or trade union. The members put their money into the union and lend it to other members. There has to be trust between the members. However, credit unions are regulated by the financial authorities and savers' deposits are protected.

The main advantages of a credit union are:

- It encourages members to save on a regular basis so they build up a pot of money.
- Members can take out a loan, usually up to £3,000 at a low rate of interest, e.g. 12–20% per year.
- It helps people to manage their money well.
- It builds community trust.

Activity

1 Which of these statements do you agree with? (You can choose more than one.)

2 Draw up an advice document to warn consumers of the dangers of payday lenders and the advantages of credit unions. You could also provide advice to help people cope if they get into trouble with payday lenders. You can find information on websites like the Citizens Advice Bureau.

> Payday lenders should be banned.

> Payday lenders provide a useful service for people who can't get money quickly elsewhere.

> The government should help set up lots of credit unions around the UK.

> Payday lenders should not be allowed to charge interest rates above … (you choose how much – 50%, 100%, 500%, 1000%, etc.).

> Payday lenders should not be allowed to 'roll over' the debt.

> Payday companies should make sure customers do not take out several loans.

> It's up to individuals to look after their own financial affairs; it's their fault if they end up paying a lot of money and get into debt.

4.5 How can I keep control of my money?

It is easy to get into debt and borrow too much. The only way to avoid this is to learn how to manage (look after) your money. You need to know how much you have coming in and how much you are spending and try to balance it. This is called budgeting. Not only does this help you avoid debt but it also helps you work out what you can afford and plan for the future.

Activity

One of the key aspects of budgeting is distinguishing between what you need and what you want.

1 Draw up a table with three columns: Needs, Wants, Not sure / it depends.
   a Put the items in the coloured ovals into one of the columns.
   b Which of these items could be a 'need' or a 'want' in different circumstances? For example, you might want a bicycle but you might also need it to get to work, or is a shirt a 'need' if you have lots in your wardrobe already?
   c Add five other 'needs' and 'wants' to your table.
2 Discuss your answers with the whole class and see if you came to the same or different conclusions.

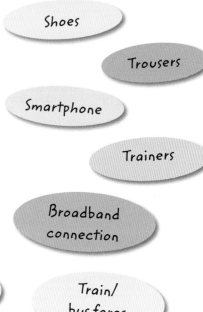

Shoes

Trousers

Smartphone

Trainers

Broadband connection

Video game/apps

A football

Music downloads

Train/ bus fares

Basic foods — meat, vegetables, etc.

Sweets/ ice cream

Refrigerator

Holiday

Bank account

Accommodation — a place to live

Activity

1 Read the information on Sam on the opposite page.
   a What is Sam's income per month?
   b What is Sam's expenditure per month?
   c What is the difference between Sam's income and expenditure?
2 What would happen if:
   • the rent was increased by £30 a month?
   • Sam lost two evenings of part-time work (£50)?
3 What could Sam do to improve the balance of the budget?
4 Suppose Sam needed £150 to pay for essential work clothes, would a credit card be the best way to do this? Explain your answer.
5 With a partner, role-play (or write) a conversation where one of you is Sam and the other is a friend giving advice on the best way to manage a budget.
6 Construct a budget of your own income and expenditure and consider the problems you have in balancing it.

Planning a budget

To plan a budget, you need to know what money you have coming in (income) and what money is going out (spending or expenditure). If you spend more than you receive in income, you will go into debt. Then you need to work out how to manage it. You can cut down your spending or work out the best way to borrow money.

Income per month	£
Wages	710
Part-time work on two evenings a week	200
Training grant	50
Total income	**£960**

Expenditure per month	£
Rent	350
Food	210
Fares to get to work	40
Gas/electricity/water	70
Clothes	50
Music downloads	15
Broadband	20
Games/films	35
Travel	30
Going out	45
Books/magazines	15
Mobile phone	25
Credit card repayments	30
Laundry	15
Total expenditure	

Balance (difference between total income and total expenditure)	

Sam

Sam, 18, has just left school and has managed to find a job. The government has provided a grant for training. Sam also has a part-time job in the evening, preparing pizzas for delivery. It's hard work.

Sam enjoys going out with friends, listening to music and gaming. The budget charts below show Sam's income and expenditure over one month.

Activity

You also use budgets for managing spending on events and projects. You have to work out what you can buy with the money you have and how you can avoid spending too much – going over budget.

Plan a budget for one of the following:

- A trip out for family or friends to a sporting event, e.g. cost of tickets, transport, food and drink.
- A party at an old folks' home or local community centre.

71

4.6 Are you a saver or a spender?

Look at the questions below and choose one answer for each. Write down a, b or c on a rough piece of paper.

1 You have got together all the money you receive for the week from your parents/other adults and any part-time jobs. Do you:
   a spend it all straightaway?
   b spend it all slowly over the week?
   c put aside some for spending and some for saving?

2 There is something you really want but don't have enough money to buy it. Do you:
   a borrow the money you need so you can get it right away?
   b get extra work, e.g. chores around the house, do a paper-round, to earn the money?
   c save up for it, even if it means waiting a while?

3 The monthly allowance of minutes on your smartphone has been used up. Do you:
   a just carry on using it because you have to stay in contact with friends, no matter what the extra costs?
   b carry on using it but cut back your use to a minimum?
   c stop using your phone till next month's allowance arrives?

4 You run out of money but need some to go out with friends. Do you:
   a borrow money from family members or friends so you can have a good time?
   b borrow a small amount and tell your friends you can only spend a limited amount of money?
   c say you can't afford to go out on this occasion?

5 You have borrowed money from friends. Do you:
   a always wait for them to ask for it back and say you'll return it when you get some spare sometime in the future?
   b pay it back in stages when you can?
   c make a point of paying it all back when you say you will?

6 You have been given some money as a present. Do you:
   a spend it all on yourself and your friends and have a great time?
   b spend some of it and keep some back for later?
   c put it straight into your savings for the future?

7 Do you like to:
   a buy things on impulse?
   b think carefully before you buy things and get the best deal?
   c make sure you can afford what you want to buy?

8 A new album from your favourite band has just been released. Do you:
   a buy it immediately online and worry about the money later?
   b wait for a friend to buy it and get the tracks you want from them?
   c buy it from your savings?

Mostly Cs – you are a saver and are cautious about spending money but you know when to spend and when to save.

Mostly Bs – you like spending but you are careful and have a healthy attitude to money.

Mostly As – you are very free with your own and other people's money. This might lead you into financial trouble in the future.

Where can you save money?

If you want to save up for something, you could put your money in a piggybank. But it would be better off in a savings account where you can earn interest on what you save. This means you get more money back than you put in. It's also useful to be able to call on savings if something happens and you suddenly need some money. It reduces the risk in managing our financial affairs.

There are a variety of different savings accounts and schemes with different advantages and disadvantages. Many of these are offered by banks, building societies and credit unions. Here are some of the main types.

Easy access accounts
You can put in your money and take it out whenever you want.

Good points
- Easy to use.
- Few restrictions of use.

Not so good
- Low rates of interest.
- Tax taken out by provider.

Notice accounts
You have to give notice before you can take money out, e.g. 30 days.

Good points
- Higher rates of interest than easy access accounts.

Not so good
- Problem if you need money quickly.
- You will lose the interest on any money you take out if you don't give notice.
- Tax taken out by provider.

NISAs (New Individual Savings Accounts)
These pay you interest tax-free. You can put in up to £15,000 (may change) in one year. You can keep the money in cash (paying a certain interest rate) or put it into stocks and shares.

Good points
- No tax.
- Investing in stocks and shares may give you back much more money.

Not so good
- Rules apply as to how you can put money in and take it out.
- If you invest in stocks and shares there is a risk – you can LOSE money.

Regular savings accounts
You put a regular amount of money in each month, e.g. £30, over a long period, e.g. a year.

Good points
- You can get a good interest rate.
- Easier to save when you put in smaller amounts regularly.

Not so good
- You pay tax on it.
- If you miss one payment, you may lose all or some of the interest.

Activity

Savings challenge
1 Using the internet, e.g. moneysavingexpert.com, find the best savings accounts for:
- A young person who has been given £1,000 and wants to be able to take it out when they want.
- An old couple who have £5,000 to save and are happy for it to stay saved for several years to get the best interest rate.
- A young person who wants to put away £20 a week.
- You. Which type of account would you use if you wanted to start saving money?
2 As you do your internet research, make notes on any advice, conditions and warnings you find on websites about savings accounts. Report these back to the class.

4.7 Being a clever consumer

Managing money is not just about borrowing, saving and budgeting, important as these are. It is also about how you spend the money you have. Shops and retailers are very good at offering all sorts of reasons for buying their goods – special deals, discounts, price reductions, buy-one-get-one-free. But these are not always what they appear and may not be good value for money. So you have to be a clever consumer.

Mobile phones

CONTRACT 1
Only £20/month for 24 months

FREE smartphone* or £50 for an upgrade

- *300 minutes*
- *200 texts*
- *1 GB data/month – FREE for first 3 months*

Other network rates:

- *Calls – 25p/min*
- *Pic msg – 35p*
- *Texts – 15p*
- *Voicemail – 40p/min*

Visit the one-stop app store and get FREE downloads: wallpaper, music, games ...

*Not latest model

Small print

CONTRACT 2
Just £40/month for 24 months

GET THE LATEST SMARTPHONE FREE

*UNLIMITED minutes + **UNLIMITED** texts!*

2GB data/month + an extra 2GB in the year you sign up. We have more apps than anyone else — and 1000s of them are free!

PAY AS YOU GO
→ *FM radio*
→ *Five built-in games*
→ *2 MPx camera*

£80

Just : 15p/min   20p/MB of data
10p/text   30p/pic msg

***TOP UP £10/month** to get 75 mins, 200 texts + 250 MB*

Activity

1 Which of these tariffs would be most suitable for:
   a you (consider how you use a phone and how much you can afford)?
   b a 19-year-old in their first job who downloads music and sends photos to friends, as well as surfing the internet (heavy usage)?
   c a person who uses their phone for business as well as friends; uses texts and Twitter frequently?
   d a pensioner – makes a few calls but uses the internet and lots of apps?
   Explain your reasons.

2 Design a mobile phone package for one of the following:
   a a person of your age
   b an 18–19-year-old
   c a 25-year-old.

3 Taking a vote in your class, see who offers:
   a the best package
   b the one likely to make the phone company the most money.

4 Why do you think some phone companies make tariffs and offers confusing?

At the shops

Retailers (people who run shops) know that people will buy things if they see money-off signs and deals. We all like to think we are getting a bargain. Some deals are good but supermarkets and shops have been criticised for misleading consumers. Also when we buy goods, there are other environmental and ethical issues to consider like the amount of packaging used and how goods are produced. For example, are these cheap clothes made by women and children in terrible conditions who earn very little? Is the chicken cheap because it has been factory farmed with no room for the chicken to move freely?

Activity

1 Look at the range of offers and deals below.
   a Decide if they are good value or not.
   b Make a list of things a person would need to take into account before purchasing them. Use the clues on this page.
2 Discuss these questions:
   a Are the more expensive items always better quality?
   b When items are really cheap, does it matter if anyone suffers?
   c Would you be prepared to pay more for goods which ensure good conditions for people and animals?

Clues

Packaging?
Convenience?
Price?
Quality?
How long will it last?
A real bargain?
Can we eat this amount?
How was this made/produced?

More is better?

Sales are good for you?

Reduced prices are good prices?

Expensive or cheap?

Bigger discounts offer better value?

5.1 What sort of country do you want to live in?

We all like to think that we live in a free country where we have the freedom to say and do what we like. But in real life we can't say and do what we like: we have to obey laws and control our behaviour because what we do affects other people. We have to balance our freedom against the laws that protect us all. Some people want more freedom and less control by the authorities; others prefer to live in countries where there are stronger laws and governments. Where do you stand on this?

Activity

1 Read the statements below and on page 77 that complete the sentence starting:

   I would prefer to live in a country where …

   and decide whether you agree, do not agree, or are not so sure about them.

2 Draw up a table like this one to record your decisions about each statement.
   Explain your thoughts on the ones you are not so sure about.

Statement	Agree	Disagree	Not sure about

3 Make a list of the five main features that you would wish to see in the society you live in, using your responses in the table.

4 Compare your list with others in the class and discuss the similarities and differences.

I would prefer to live in a country where …

A … there are regular elections to choose the people who are going to run the country.

B … the government has a lot of control over what is shown on TV or printed in the newspapers.

C … only men are allowed to vote.

D … people can follow any religion they like.

E … newspapers and magazines can print any stories they like about people's private lives.

F … the police do exactly what the government tells them.

G … everyone can get together to discuss their views or hold meetings.

H … people are allowed to protest and demonstrate if they don't like what the government is doing.

I … people have complete freedom of speech.

J … the government keeps lots of information about everyone in a database to protect people from terrorism.

K … everybody has the right to a trial by a jury of their fellow citizens.

L … everyone obeys the laws, including members of the government.

M … if people are arrested they have to be told why, and if they are charged there must be a trial.

N … people have the right to see any records or documents that the government, local councils, schools and hospitals have on them.

O … the police have all the powers they need to protect people from terrorism, such as entering houses without permission, listening in on telephone calls and holding people for questioning.

P … the government controls judges and the courts of law.

R … the government is allowed to keep what it does secret.

Q … people are allowed to say things that are racist or offend another person's religion.

S … the people's representatives can question the government to check what it is doing, and to make sure it is not corrupt and is acting properly.

T … religion has no role in the way a country is governed.

U … people who protest against the government and cause trouble in the streets are put in prison.

V … people have the right to meet together to discuss their views.

Democracy

It is very likely that most of the statements you agreed with in the activity on the previous two pages make up features of what we call 'democracy'. You can see a definition of democracy on the right, although not everybody agrees about what the word democracy means. This is because it is very difficult to create a system in which people have a say in running or 'governing' a country. Democracies around the world are run differently. In the UK, we elect 'representatives' to speak for the people. But elections are not enough. We could elect a leader and government who treat people badly. To avoid this, most democracies share a belief in the basic principles below.

> **Definition of democracy**
> 'Government of the people, by the people, for the people.'

Three basic principles of democracy

1 Freedom of speech, belief and association (joining groups) for everyone.
2 The rule of law and everyone is equal under the law.
3 The government represents the people of the country and is accountable to the people of that country.

Activity

The aim of this activity is to help you think about what the basic principles of democracy mean.

1 Draw up a table like the one shown below:

Government represents people and is accountable	The rule of law and everybody is equal under the law	Freedom of speech, belief and association
The actions of the government have to be made public and explained, so that people can check what they are doing.	The judges and courts are not controlled by the government.	The press, TV and radio should not be censored by the government.

2 Take the statements from pages 76–77 and put them in the appropriate column of the chart. You will have to re-write some of the statements. For instance, Statement P should be re-written to say the government should **not** control judges and the courts in a democracy. It then goes into the 'rule of law' column (shown as an example in the table).

3 Discuss in class any different opinions about the statements and which principle they fit into.

Freedom

There is a long history in this country of people fighting for their different rights and liberties. You can see some of the main ones below. We see these freedoms as an essential part of our democracy. In some countries in the world today, people have few rights and little freedom. They can be imprisoned without a trial and then tortured, or even killed, especially if they disagree with the government.

However, our freedom is not something that we should take for granted. It can easily be lost. Being allowed to campaign to protect certain freedoms is one of the features of a free society. People do disagree, however, about which freedoms should be protected, especially when society is under threat. We are going to look at some areas where people disagree on the next few pages.

> **Definition of freedom**
> 'The right to act, think or speak as you want, without interference from a despotic government'.

The right to vote and choose a government in elections

Free speech and a free press

Freedom of opinion, conscience, belief and religion

Freedom to protest

The right to an education

Freedom to join organisations like political parties and trade unions

Freedom to own property

The right to a fair trial if arrested and to know what you are being arrested for

Freedom of movement, to go where you want, leave a country

Activity

1   Work in pairs. Draw a diamond shape like the one shown on the right. Arrange the statements above in order of the ones you prize most. Put the one you think is the most valuable at the top, the next two on the next line and so on.

    Be prepared to give your reasons for your choices.

2   Compare these with others in the class and discuss what you think these freedoms/rights mean.

3   Can you see any issues that might be thrown up by any of these when putting them into practice in a society?

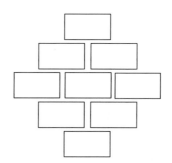

5.3 Conflicting rights

Free countries support human rights. They also have other laws, which are not always the same as human rights, to protect people from any abuse of power by the government of that country. These rights are called civil liberties. Not all free countries have the same civil liberties. For example, in the USA, people see the right to carry guns ('bear arms') as a civil liberty, but this is not the case in the UK, where there are strict laws controlling who is allowed to carry a gun.

Living in a society where rights are guaranteed leads some people to think they have the freedom to behave exactly as they wish, even though their behaviour might offend or inconvenience other people. We need to think about how to balance one person's rights against another person's freedoms. The law tries to protect everyone's rights, but sometimes there is disagreement. For example, the debate about whether or not people should be allowed to smoke in public led to a law forbidding it.

> **Definition of human rights**
>
> 'Human rights are basic rights that everyone is entitled to expect and that all human beings should have, no matter where in the world they live. Examples are the right to life, freedom from torture and freedom from slavery'.

Activity

1 In pairs, look at the situations below and on page 81. Decide whether you agree with each person.

2 When you have decided which people you agree with, join up with another pair and see if you all feel the same way.

3 Choose two situations where you think the person has a good case and decide what should happen. Your teacher can tell you the legal position in each situation.

A Jo Cheung is a keen supporter of animal rights. She intends to demonstrate in a big rally that has been planned outside a research laboratory. The police have decided to cancel the rally because of threats of violence and risks to the safety of workers at the laboratory. Jo says the right to protest is a precious liberty being denied by the police.

B Sunil Khan and his neighbours are fed up with the noise of aeroplanes flying over their neighbourhood; they are on a flight path. On some days they are woken up at six in the morning and there are also some night flights. Health reports have shown that lack of sleep is a health risk. The constant noise certainly makes their quality of life worse. They want to see flights restricted and say they have the right to a good night's sleep. The airport authorities say that they just have to put up with it because the airport is good for the economy and therefore everyone.

C **Jane Simpson** has written a magazine article about people who come from a particular country. It is a very critical article and says some very unpleasant things. The editor of the magazine says he will not publish the article because it would offend people. Jane argues that she has a right to freedom of expression, to say what she believes to be the truth.

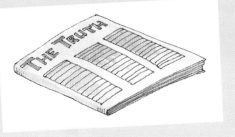

D **Maroula Mitchell** has found out that her employer has been monitoring her emails to her boyfriend from the company computer. The employer says she is wasting time at work, which he is paying her for, but Maroula says she has a right to privacy and to communicate with friends if she wishes.

E **Rob Jansen** loves music and likes to listen to it wherever he is. He has a mobile phone that plays music and sometimes he wants to listen to it out loud and not just through earphones. One day when he is listening to his music on the bus, a woman in the seat behind says that she does not want to hear his music and would prefer him to use his earphones.

F **Maureen Bell** owns a shop in the high street. The shop is always being targeted by shoplifters and she wants the police to install more security cameras in the street outside her shop. A local civil liberties group says that there are already too many cameras in the high street and strongly opposes the request. They say it is becoming like a police state where everybody is being spied on all the time.

5.4 How free should the press be?

Many people say that they prefer to live in a country where there is freedom to say or write what you think, and that this is particularly important for newspapers. In this country, we say that we have press freedom. But people disagree about whether newspapers have too much or not enough freedom, and some people would like to see more controls put on the press.

The importance of a free press

When we talk about putting controls on the press, we have to be very careful. Press freedom is essential to democracy. In the UK the government cannot tell the newspapers what they are allowed to print. This means we can hear a variety of opinions on different issues and we don't only hear one side. A free press performs a number of useful functions:

● It provides information so that we are able to make informed judgements about issues.
● The press keeps an eye on the government to make sure that it is not misleading the public about its policies and provides comment. It also tells us what our government is doing in other countries.
● It exposes corruption in government or business.
● It uncovers injustice where the people have been treated unfairly by the government, the law or powerful people and companies.

Activity

The Daily Telegraph

BRITAIN'S BEST-SELLING QUALITY DAILY

The truth about the Cabinet's expenses

the guardian

The Whistleblower

THE SUNDAY TIMES

Our Thalidomide Children

Look at these examples of press exposures. Take each one in turn and explain how it shows that a free investigative press is vital to democracy in different areas of life.

● The *Telegraph* revealed the scandal around the way MPs' expenses were claimed. Some were claiming living expenses in houses that they were actually renting out. Newspapers also found out that some MPs were being paid money to ask questions in Parliament.
● The *Guardian* printed information from a whistleblower in the USA, which showed that British and American intelligence agencies were monitoring people's emails.
● The *Sunday Times* exposed the scandal of the drug Thalidomide which was being prescribed for morning sickness in pregnant women but was causing babies to be born with disabilities. The paper campaigned for damages to be paid to the victims.

When the press is not free

Countries that deny basic human rights often deny people press freedom as well. People who speak out or write in newspapers criticising the government of their country can be arrested and imprisoned. Dictatorships or authoritarian governments do not want their citizens to find out or question what they are doing. They may be killing or imprisoning people or making decisions which may be having a detrimental effect on the population. Similarly, there are powerful people who may be negotiating business deals, perhaps involving bribery and corruption, who do not want people to find out what they are doing. It is usually only the actions of brave journalists who investigate and challenge these people that bring their wrongdoings to light.

Yang Tongyan, who opposed the Chinese government's treatment of protestors at Tiananmen Square in 1989, wrote articles for US-based websites about abuses of human rights in China. In 2006 he was sentenced to 12 years imprisonment for 'subverting state authority'. Relatives who visited Yang in prison in 2012 said he was receiving poor treatment for a number of medical conditions including tuberculosis, arthritis, and diabetes.

Anabel Hernández is a Mexican journalist known for her investigative reporting on corruption and abuse of power in politics. She was recognised by UNICEF for uncovering slave labour networks. She has received numerous death threats for detailing the relationship between organised crime and high level government, police, military and other officials. Anabel now lives and works protected by bodyguards.

Iryna Khalip, a Belarusian journalist, has been harassed, beaten and put in prison for criticising the dictatorial government of President Alexander Lukashenko. She says, 'Dictatorships don't like journalists – they either destroy them or buy them out.' A number of Iryna's fellow journalists have been murdered and she has received death threats. However, she has said that she won't stop reporting on civil and human rights abuses.

Activity

1 Explain the reasons why some powerful people in politics, business and crime might be frightened of a free press.

2 With a partner, discuss the reasons why journalists like Anabel, Yang and Iryna would take such huge risks in what they choose to investigate and report.

How free should the press be in the UK?

A free press is an important aspect of a free society. But do newspapers sometimes go too far in their search for stories to attract their readers' interest? People have a right to privacy. However, sometimes there is a public interest in revealing what people do in private.

The problem is that it can be very difficult to decide exactly what 'public interest' means. It does not simply mean that the public are interested. The public – the readers of newspapers and watchers of television – are interested in most things about people, particularly their relationships and their sex lives. 'Public interest' is when it is important to know something about someone because they are public figures or because what they do affects other people.

So how far should the press go? When do we have the right to know about the private life of a politician, celebrity or ordinary member of the public, if at all?

The hacking scandal

Discussions about the role of the press in a free society came to a head with the 'hacking scandal' in 2012–2013. The employees of a number of newspapers, particularly the *News of the World*, were accused of illegally hacking into the voicemails of mobile phones in order to find newsworthy stories. A wide range of people were affected: celebrities, members of the royal family, politicians and the families of victims of crime and tragedy.

There were also accusations of journalists bribing the police for tip-offs about stories. The *News of the World* was eventually closed and several senior staff members at that paper and others were charged with offences.

In the scandal that followed, a public inquiry under Lord Justice Leveson was set up to look at press abuses and ways of controlling the press when it goes too far. The inquiry revealed many examples of situations where the press had intruded into people's private lives and had caused them upset and distress. There were claims that the press had hounded and harassed people and printed false stories. There were no real penalties if editors or journalists broke the press code of practice. This was because the newspapers themselves were their own regulator and people with a complaint had to report any misconduct to them.

Activity

1 Consider the viewpoints about the press in the coloured ovals below.
   - Which of them argue for press freedom and which for more control of the press?
   - Would you make a difference between famous people (politicians, public figures, celebrities) and the ordinary public? Should different groups of people be treated differently by the press?
   - Which of the viewpoints do you agree with?
2 Using all the information on pages 82–85, write a blog with the title: 'The freedom of the press is vital to a healthy democracy'.

A
The freedom of the press is so important to democracy that it is better that there are very few controls, even if sometimes the newspapers go too far.

B
Newspapers dig into people's private lives and print stories that cause a lot of distress. Quite often these stories have no real 'public interest'.

C
If you bring in any laws or big penalties to control the press, then powerful politicians and businessmen will use them to stop newspapers revealing information about them we need to know.

D
The laws of this country are strong enough already to protect people. You can always sue in the courts.

E
Famous people should expect people to be interested in their lives. Some of them seek out publicity to get attention.

F
We need a tough regulator – a group of people that can impose penalties on the press – large fines and apologies if they have unfairly intruded upon people's lives.

5.5 Who's watching you?

Privacy is an important right in our everyday lives, but it is now possible to track ordinary people wherever they go. Technology is making it easier all the time for the authorities to pinpoint where people are and what they are doing. Also, the government, the police and big companies hold a lot of information on us; and often we give away information about ourselves on internet social networking sites. Some people say all this is a threat to our privacy and our civil liberties.

Mobile phones

Sophisticated devices can listen in to mobile phone conversations. Even when the phone is on stand-by, it is in contact with the base station, telling it where you and the phone are. Phones with GPS can even tell others what kinds of shops, restaurants, clubs or places of worship you are visiting.

MY-MOBILE
THE MOBILE PHONE COMPANY

MS SAM BROWN
42 HOVE ROAD
BRIGHTON

MOBILE PHONE NUMBER
07291 654321

STATEMENT

LOCATION	DATE	TIME	DURATION	NUMBER	AMOUNT
CAMBRIDGE	15.03.10	13.50	4.02	07304 123456	£0.52

Credit and debit cards

Paying by card shows where you have been and what you have bought. Taking cash out of an ATM provides a record of where that card has been used and how much money has been taken out.

SECURITY CAMERA 6783   09:00   15.03.10

CCTV

Many towns and cities have closed circuit television (CCTV) cameras which record people as they go about their daily lives. In shops, trains, stations and offices, CCTV cameras film people moving around. Cameras on the motorway and in high streets record the cars travelling, what speed they are doing and where they are parked. The number plate can be recognised by automatic number recognition (ANR) camera systems, so you can identify the owner of the car. Face recognition systems are being introduced.

Email and internet

Computers keep a record of internet sites you have visited. It is possible to detect these even if the pages on the internet site are deleted or you clear the history of websites visited. Emails are often intercepted for security checks, and intelligence services know who receives and sends the messages. What's more, many people put personal information on their public Facebook pages, forgetting that these pages can be accessed by anyone in the world and that the information exists forever.

Information held by organisations

All the government departments have information on us, including the Inland Revenue (tax collection), the vehicle and driving licence offices, the police, the benefits office and the local authority. Increasingly, information from social networking sites is being used by the police, insurance companies and employers. People who use loyalty cards in supermarkets are sometimes surprised to find out that their shopping habits are tracked so that they can be targeted with adverts for particular goods.

A They have forgotten to take some essential medicine, without which they will become very ill.

B The intelligence services suspect them of belonging to a terrorist organisation that may be planning to explode a bomb.

C Their partner suspects them of having an affair and the partner has employed a private detective.

D They are part of a group that disagrees with the government and is planning to hold a peaceful demonstration outside Parliament.

E A robbery has taken place and they are suspected of being involved.

F They have gone missing from home and the family is worried about them.

Activity

1 Sometimes people need to be located quickly and sometimes they have a right not to be located. Think about the situations in the boxes on this page. When should someone be found and when should their right to privacy be protected?

2 Do you think that having so many CCTV cameras on the streets to watch people and vehicles is good for society or not?

3 What are the problems of governments holding a huge amount of information about us?

4 Do you think any controls should be brought in to stop companies tracking us on computers and collecting information about us, especially to target advertising at us?

5.6 The freedom to protest

One of the most important principles of our democracy is the right of people to disagree with the elected government and peacefully protest about the things they disagree with. Peaceful protests allow people to come together and stand up for what they believe in. Protest can take a number of forms.

▲ Boycotts

▲ Petitions

▲ Letters to Members of Parliament (MPs) or government ministers

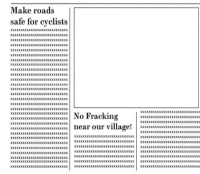

▲ Letters to newspapers

▲ Stunts

▲ Demonstrations: sit-ins, marches, rallies, picketing

▲ Advertisements in newspapers, on TV, on posters or leaflets

▲ Strikes

▲ Performances: satire, comedy, theatre, songs

Protest marches

Anyone organising a march is legally required to notify the police six days in advance so that they can warn people using the route. Protesters are not obliged to notify the police if the demonstration is a protest rally, but it helps avoid confrontation if they do.

Sometimes, what starts as peaceful protest becomes violent. Police have many legal powers that can be used to prevent violent protest. They can limit the march, ask for a change of location or duration of a rally. They do this in order to prevent public disorder, damage to property or disruption. Police might carry out stop and search operations at a protest meeting but they must say on what legal grounds they are doing it. A sit-down protest can be stopped if it blocks the highway and any racist chants or threats could lead to arrest of those involved.

Activity

1   If you wanted to bring about a change, which methods of peaceful protest would you choose? Look at the issues below. Select two and explain which methods you would use and why. Or choose an issue that you think is important.

   ● An unsafe railway level crossing

   ● Safer cycle routes

   ● Environment disaster, e.g. oil polluting the sea or 'fracking' causing damage underground

   ● Modern day slavery and human trafficking

2   What causes do you think each of these three images is linked to? How have we benefited from these causes today?

5.7 The right to education

In this country, every child has a right to an education. This was a right hard-won during the nineteenth century, when many children had to work in often appalling conditions to contribute to family income. Once a law was passed in 1870, stating that all children had to attend school, it was no longer possible for parents or employers to put young children out to work.

In some countries, education is still not available for all children – it is either too expensive or not considered appropriate for some. In Pakistan, for example, the Taliban (an Islamic fundamentalist movement) has tried to stop girls from attending school.

One such girl is Malala Yousafzai, from the Swat District in Pakistan. She has campaigned for girls' education from an early age. When she was only eleven, she wrote a blog for the BBC, talking about her everyday life under Taliban rule and promoting education for girls. A film about her views was broadcast in America. In 2012, when Malala was fifteen, she was shot in the head by a gunman while returning home on a school bus, in an attempt to silence her.

She was unconscious for many days and was eventually sent from Pakistan to a hospital in Birmingham, where she had several operations and made a good recovery. As a result of her brave campaign for girls' education, she was asked to speak at the United Nations, on her sixteenth birthday.

She has strong views about how young people should regard their education. In a television interview, she said:

Malala Yousafzai

'I want to tell the students of UK to think that it is very precious, it's very prestigious, to go to school. Reading a book, having a pen in our hands, studying, sitting in a classroom is something very special for us because once we were deprived from it and because what we have seen in Swat … When I was born, some of our relatives came to our house and told my mother, "Don't worry, next time you will have a son"…

▲ Malala Yousafzai speaking at the United Nations.

For my brothers it was easy to think about the future, they can be anything they want. But for me it was hard and for that reason, I wanted to become educated and I wanted to empower myself with knowledge.'

Activity

1   Should children in the UK still have to go to school if they don't want to? As a class, survey your views and find out how many think that school should not be compulsory at all, how many think school should be compulsory until 14, until 16 and until 18.

2   What arguments would you use to persuade young people who do not want to go to school that education is important and valuable in a free society? Malala's interview may help you think about this.

3   Why do some people in some parts of the world want to stop girls getting an education?

Would you speak out?

Malala showed great courage when she continued to argue for girls' education, even when she nearly died as a result of speaking out. In Britain, we like to believe that we have the right to say what we believe in, without fear of violence or intimidation.

But do we all use that freedom? What about you? There are lots of times when you might be called upon to express a view, tell the truth, fight for a cause that you believe in or go against some of your friends. What would you do?

Activity

Work in pairs and decide what you would do in each of the following situations. You can choose: 'Speak out', 'Stay silent' or 'It depends …' (but you must say what it depends on).

1. Stand up for someone who is being bullied by your friends.

2. Tell someone you know, even an adult, that you don't like them making racist jokes.

3. Defend someone who you think has been treated unjustly at school.

4. Identify someone who you know is guilty of an attack on someone else.

5. Write a letter to a newspaper supporting a cause that you feel really strongly about.

6. Take part in a local campaign to save a facility such as a library or a nursery school.

7. Agree to be a witness in a court case if you have seen a crime being committed.

8. Argue an unpopular point of view in a debate.

6.1 A brief history of parliamentary democracy

Our parliamentary democracy has taken shape over hundreds of years. It has not always been a peaceful process and has involved wars, violent protest and civil disobedience, as well as debate, argument, goodwill and tolerance. The end result is the system we have today which includes some strange elements like the traditions of parliament (e.g. Black Rod) and the existence of a House of Lords. Some people say that it is this which has given democracy in the UK its special character. The timeline contains some of the key points and events in its history.

Origin of word 'parliament'

A meeting to discuss matters, from the French word 'parler' (to talk). Early parliaments in Britain were often about 'talking' to help kings make decisions.

The Witan

Anglo-Saxon kings called on the Witan, a council of leading advisors and nobles, for advice.

Activity

1 Choose one of the following:

   a Make your own diagram of the timeline with notes.
   b Draw a storyboard of 6–8 scenes/slides with captions showing key points in the history of Parliament (or use computer software like Movie Maker).
   c Imagine you had to describe how the UK Parliament developed to a person from another country. Write a brief and simple description, explaining how Parliament became more democratic and why there is a House of Lords and a House of Commons.
2 Different groups in the class can research key events in more detail and present their findings in a short presentation.

Monarchs in control

After 1066, medieval monarchs had a 'Great Council' of the most powerful lords (forerunner to the House of Lords) to advise them. But kings made all the key decisions.

Magna Carta 1215

Powerful barons and nobles forced King John to sign the Magna Carta (Great Charter) in 1215. Its aim was to restrict the power of the king. It also stated that freemen could not be put in prison without a trial.

Simon de Montfort's Parliament

Simon de Montfort – and the leading barons – who had defeated Henry III in battle, called his own parliament in 1265 to help him run the country. This included not only powerful lords (barons and bishops) but also representatives from counties and large towns. It is seen as the first step to our modern Parliament.

Rise of the Commons

Edward III (1327-77) held regular parliaments because he needed to raise taxes. He also called representatives from counties (knights) and towns (mainly rich merchants) to attend. They sat separately from the king and his nobles in one chamber which became known as the House of Commons.

Pocket boroughs

Some boroughs (towns that elected MPs) were called 'pocket boroughs' because powerful aristocrats were able, by bribing or threatening people, to send the MPs they chose to the House of Commons. E.g., the Duke of Newcastle was said to have seven boroughs under his control ('in his pocket').

Rotten boroughs

Other boroughs were called 'rotten boroughs' because only a few people elected an MP to Parliament.

The eighteenth century

Parliament was becoming powerful but was not democratic. The aristocracy, the great landowners (from whom the Lords came), controlled much of the House of Commons through corruption. The number of voters at this time was small because you had to own property of a certain value to be able to vote. Also the ballot was not secret so people knew who you vote for.

The Glorious Revolution 1688

Parliament invited William of Orange to replace James II, an unpopular king. William's powers were limited by the 1689 Bill of Rights. He was a 'constitutional monarch' and had to get Parliament's approval of his policies. Powers to do with making laws and the finances of the nation were handed over to Parliament. The King had to ask Parliament for any money he needed.

OLIVER CROMWELL

CHARLES I

Civil War 1642-49

By the seventeenth century, Parliament had become a powerful body, especially the Commons. When King Charles I tried to rule without the support of Parliament, events led to civil war. This was a struggle over power, money and religion. Parliament won and Charles was executed in 1649. For a short time the country was a republic under Oliver Cromwell. But the monarchy was restored in 1660.

Kings always needed money and parliaments were useful because kings could get their help in raising taxes. This gave Members of Parliament (MPs) the opportunity to petition the king and discuss complaints and grievances.

Growing influence

Throughout the fourteenth century, the Lords and the Commons wanted to have their views about the running of the country taken into account by the monarch. It became accepted that new taxes could not be raised unless Parliament agreed. The House of Lords was far more powerful than the Commons. By the end of the fifteenth century, the Lords had established the right to hand on their seat in the House of Lords to their heirs. They were 'hereditary peers'.

Nineteenth-century changes

Huge changes were taking place in Britain at the beginning of the nineteenth century. Industrialisation was creating towns and cities with large populations. Ideas of freedom and democracy were coming from the French and American revolutions. People were not prepared to see Parliament controlled by rich landowners. They wanted the vote so that Parliament represented them and became more democratic.

The Great Reform Act, 1832

Middle-class men who owned property (well-off) were now able to vote (around half a million men). Some of the rotten and pocket boroughs controlled by the aristocracy were got rid of, so the House of Lords had less control of the MPs in the House of Commons. But only a minority of the population could vote.

The
PEOPLE's
CHARTER

1. One man one vote
2. Voting in secret
3. MPs don't have to own property
4. MPs to be paid
5. Equal sizes of constituencies
6. Annual elections

The Chartists, 1834–48

Working-class men demanded a People's Charter which included votes for men over 21 who did not own property and a secret ballot. They staged petitions, marches and protests. The movement failed but most of their demands were put into practice later.

The Second Reform Act, 1867

More men were given the vote (2.5 million out of 22 million adult male population).

The 1872 Ballot Act

Secret ballot introduced for elections.

The Third Reform Act 1884

Working men were given the vote (two-thirds of the male population could vote). The House of Commons was now much more representative of the population and power was shifting from the Lords to the Commons. Cities and towns with larger populations were given more MPs.

Devolution

In 1997–99, powers were transferred from the UK Parliament in Westminster to separate parliaments in Scotland (Scottish Parliament), Wales (National Assembly for Wales) and the Northern Ireland Assembly. They have powers over a range of issues, e.g. education and health, and are to make laws in these areas. Other powers such as defence and foreign policy have been retained by the Westminster Parliament.

Europe, 1973 to present

In 1973, the UK joined the Common Market in Europe. This evolved into the European Union, which bound countries together in a tighter set of rules, regulations and understandings. The UK government and Parliament has to follow these and many UK laws now have their origins in the EU.

Some people believe our membership of the European Union (EU) has damaged our Parliamentary democracy because we cannot make our own laws and run our own affairs freely without EU interference.

House of Lords Reform 1999

Most of the hereditary peers had their right to sit in the House of Lords removed. Ninety-two peers were allowed to carry on sitting until further reform of the House. An appointments committee was set up to choose life peers (see page 118).

Votes for women

Women mounted a long campaign for the vote from 1900 onwards. The Suffragettes used violent tactics to gain publicity.

1918

Women over the age of 30 got the vote (8.5 million) and so did all men over 21.

1928

All women over the age of 21 could vote.

The Lords v Commons 1911

The struggle between the House of Lords and the House of Commons came to a head at the beginning of the twentieth century when the Lords rejected a number of Bills and a budget which had been passed by the House of Commons. The Commons would not stand for this and forced through the Parliament Act of 1911, which reduced the power of the House of Lords. The Lords could only delay Bills becoming law for two years (reduced to one year in 1949). The Lords could not interfere with taxation matters and anything to do with money.

6.2 What role does the monarchy play in the UK?

Monarchy (being ruled by a king or queen) is one of the oldest forms of government. Traditionally, monarchs claimed that their right to rule had been given to them by God. Most countries in the world have got rid of their monarchies and become republics. Some, like Britain, have become constitutional monarchies where the monarchs have given up most of their power to parliaments elected by the people. We have seen how this happened on pages 92–95.

Our monarch is the 'head of state' and has a number of jobs. The monarch:

- opens and closes Parliament
- gives royal assent to new laws
- after an election, asks the party that has the most MPs to form a government
- meets leaders of other countries
- is the symbolic head of the Commonwealth
- hands out honours.

The monarch is also a symbol of Great Britain and a figurehead for the nation.

C

D

A

B

E

Activity

The photographs on page 96 and this page show the monarch playing different roles in our society and fulfilling different functions. Take each photograph in turn and either:

a describe the role she is playing, or

b explain how she is a symbol or figurehead.

F

G

H

I

6.3 Is it time for the monarchy to change?

The future of the monarchy in our society is an important issue to debate as we move further into the twenty-first century. In recent years the monarchy has become very popular, so some people would like to keep it as it is. Some would like to keep the monarchy but change its role in a modern society. Others would like to see this country become a republic. You are going to debate this. Before you do so, read pages 100–101: Developing your arguing skills.

Different views on money and the monarchy

Activity

Divide the class up into three main groups with smaller groups within each one. The three groups take one of these positions:

1 Keep the monarchy as it is.
2 Get rid of the monarchy and make Britain a republic.
3 Change the monarchy.

Take some time for each group to prepare their arguments using some of the points suggested below and on page 99. You can use any of these points but you might have to change them to fit your argument (i.e. turn them around to say the opposite). You can also research more arguments on the internet.

Debate the motion: We can no longer accept the monarchy in its present form.

The monarchy brings a huge amount of money to this country through tourism. The royal palaces and the parades and ceremonies are a major tourist attraction.

The monarch pays taxes, so some of the money comes from them.

There are lots of members of the royal family whom we don't really know much about. We pay for their upkeep too.

The monarchy may bring in money through tourism. But what you have conveniently left out is how much the monarchy costs taxpayers. Millions of pounds of our money goes to pay for the upkeep of the palaces, for royal visits, ceremonies and banquets.

We could just keep the monarch and a few members of the royal family but not pay for all the others and reduce the number of palaces.

Different views on democracy, power and the monarchy

> The monarchy is not democratic; nobody voted for them. A monarch becomes a king or queen by accident of birth. It would be better to have an elected head of state.

> Actually, the monarchy is more popular than most politicians who are elected. If there was a vote, the majority of people would vote for them.

> A president is often elected by about half the people in a country, so may not have everybody's support. The monarch, chosen by accident of birth, is not associated with any political side or political views, so everybody can support them.

> How do you know this? You've just made it up. What evidence do you have for saying most people would vote to keep the monarchy?

> Your argument is not logical. Most people elected the president, even if it's not all the people. To jump to the idea that 'accident of birth' is better does not make sense.

> The monarchy acts as a symbol of national unity in difficult times. Everybody can unite behind them, whatever political party they support. The monarch is neutral and does not side with any political party. It gives our country stability.

> I agree that people can unite behind the monarchy but there is no reason why a president or prime minister cannot be a unifying force during a war or crisis. This happens in other countries, like the USA.

Different views on fairness, equality and the monarchy

> Having a royal family creates a system where some people are seen as better than others. Why should we have lords and ladies who are supposed to be better than ordinary people? Our society should be more equal.

> I completely disagree. The monarchy is central to our heritage and traditions. It is an important part of what makes us British. People like to see ceremonies and parades and our society would be poorer without them. Also, people should be rewarded for their contribution to society by getting medals and other honours.

> The system of honours with medals and knighthoods, given out by the monarch, is unfair. Most of the important honours go to the rich and powerful, making them even more powerful.

Developing your arguing skills

To be an effective citizen you need to be able to put your point of view across to other people. This means that you need to argue your case by giving reasons for your views. You need to make clear points and support these by providing evidence or further explanation. We call this 'reasoned argument'.

Activity

You can read examples of the four types of challenge below in the arguments about the monarchy on pages 98–99. Find an example of each one.

Example

Point

It is important to keep the monarchy because the king or queen can unify the country in difficult times.

Reason

The monarch does not side with any political party and does not get involved in political arguments. So in times of crisis, the people of the UK can unite behind the monarch. This is particularly true in times of war or economic depression when people might lose trust in politicians or there might be disagreements between different political groups.

Counter-argument

When you debate with others you have to learn the skill of responding to what people say and challenging their arguments. Sometimes this involves simply putting across the opposite point of view but a more effective way is to find things wrong with their argument. Here are four ways of doing this:

1 Challenge the speaker directly. Ask the speaker to provide evidence for their views or challenge their evidence. Examples are:
- 'What evidence do you have for saying that?'
- 'I don't trust the source of your evidence, it's a biased source.'
- 'The figures I have contradict yours.'

2 Some arguments don't make sense – they are not logical. Point this out to the speaker. For example:
- 'There is something wrong with what you're saying. It does not make sense ...'

Challenging the arguments of others

3 Sometimes people leave out important bits of an argument. Point out what they are leaving out. For example:
- 'I do not think you have given us the full story. What you have not said is ...'

4 Accept part of the argument of your opponent but not all of it. For example:
- 'I agree with the first part of what you say, but not the rest of your argument.'

Speaking persuasively

There are a number of techniques to persuade people to agree with your viewpoint. Here are several:

- Use **persuasive words** such as *surely*, *obviously*, *undoubtedly*, e.g. 'it is undoubtedly the case that ...'

- Use **emotive words** to create sympathy or affect emotions such as *noble*, *tortured*, *cruel*, *wise*, e.g. 'these animals were tortured in experiments ...'

- Make people **feel guilty** if they don't accept your argument or appeal to their better nature, e.g. 'could you stand by and watch the suffering caused by ...'

- Find an **expert** who supports your views, e.g. 'Professor Green, this country's leading authority, says ...'

- Suggest that it is a **popular view**, e.g. 'most people agree with me when I say ...'

- Suggest that there is some sort of **threat or doom**, e.g. 'if we don't deal with knife crime now, it will not be safe for people to go out at night ...'

- Make them believe there are **only two options**, your one or an unattractive one, e.g. 'you either give people the right to die or condemn them to live out the rest of their lives in great pain ...'

Other tips

- Vary the tone of your voice and sometimes speak louder and sometimes softer. Don't go on monotonously in the same tone.

- Get your body language right. Stand upright, look straight ahead and look confident.

- Keep your audience's attention.

  - Make eye contact.
  - Don't read directly from a book or sheet of paper.
  - Try to look only briefly at your notes and keep looking at the audience.
  - Use humour if you can or put in a little story.

The Government

The Prime Minister (PM) is the head of the Government which runs the country. He or she is the head of the armed forces and represents the UK in international affairs, working with other world leaders.

The Cabinet

The Prime Minister chooses a group of people to help run the country, called the Cabinet. They are the most important ministers in the government who are in charge of big departments such as:

- the Foreign and Commonwealth Office (relations with other countries)
- the Home Office (law and order, police, courts)
- health (hospitals, medical services).

Under the Cabinet are around 100 other government ministers who help run all the departments which get things done in the country. See page 124 for more on the Cabinet.

Civil servants

The people who work in these departments – many thousands of them – are called civil servants. Their job is to carry out the instructions of government ministers and put the government's policies and ideas into practice.

For example, if the Cabinet decides to build more hospitals and schools, civil servants have to make sure this happens.

The House of Commons

There are 650 MPs who get a 'seat' in the House of Commons.

The political party which wins the most seats usually forms the government. The leader of this party becomes the Prime Minister.

The House of Commons:

- makes laws
- questions the government and examines what it is doing
- keeps a check on the amount of money that the government spends.

General Elections

(See pages 107–09.)
Elections must he held every five years. The United Kingdom has 650 constituencies which vary in size but contain on average about 69,000 people. One MP is elected for each constituency.

Any British citizen over the age of 18 can vote, although some people are excluded, e.g. members of the House of Lords or certain prisoners.

Head of State

King or Queen

(See pages 96–97 for the role of the monarch.)

In theory the monarch has no real power but he or she does have influence. This could be very significant in a time of crisis.

The House of Lords

There are around 800 members (called 'peers') who have seats in the House of Lords.
They are made up of life peers and hereditary peers (see page 118).

The main role of the House of Lords is to:

- act as a check on the House of Commons to make sure that new laws are discussed thoroughly and not rushed through
- look critically at the work of the government
- hold debates on important issues.

The Judiciary

This is independent of government.

UK courts of law

Their main function is to uphold the law. Judges are chosen by senior judges, not the government. The highest court is the Supreme Court, which:

- is the final court of appeal for civil and criminal cases in the UK
- hears appeals on points of law of general public importance
- can hold the government to account if it does not act within the law
- cannot quash laws made by Parliament.

VOTE HERE

Activity

1 What are the main 'checks and balances' in the British system? 'Checks and balances' means:
   - the ways that the power of the Government can be checked and scrutinised (looked at closely) so that it does not become too powerful
   - making sure that no one part of the system can become too powerful
   - making sure that the law and courts are not controlled by the Government or politicians.

2 Draw your own chart or diagram to show how the British system of parliamentary government works. Use illustrations or notes to make it more interesting.

6.5 Political parties

One way of getting your views heard in a democracy is by joining or supporting a political party. A political party is an organised group of people with a leader and members. It has a particular set of views and beliefs. People join the party because they agree with what it stands for. Parties put up **candidates** at elections so that these people can be voted into positions of power. If they win the election then the party can put its ideas into practice.

Activity

You are going to create your own political party.

1 Work in groups of four or five. Imagine that you want to make this country a better place in which to live. What would you change?

In your group, choose three things that you would like to change. You can get some ideas from this page, or you can come up with some of your own.

Improve the environment

Build more houses for people

Cut down crime

Control the bankers and banks

Cut the amount of money spent on the welfare system

Make the health service better

Make sure more young people can get jobs

Stop people claiming benefits they are not entitled to

Bring in laws to protect animals

Bring in measures to lessen the impact of climate change

Improve schools and the education system

Improve the railways and road system

Help poorer people in the rest of the world

Provide more social services to help people

Activity

2 Give your party a name and elect a leader.

Our party is suggesting a number of ways to improve the environment in which we all live.

3 Draw a table like the one below and fill it in. (The completed row is just an example to help you.)

  a In the first column put the three issues you have chosen.

  b Then decide what you want to do about these issues. These are your **aims**. Put these in the second column.

  c Decide how you are going to do it. These are your **policies**. Put these in the third column.

Name of our party:		
Our three issues	**What we want to achieve (our aims)**	**How we can do it (our policies)**
Make sure young people can get jobs	• Provide more courses to give young people the skills they need to do jobs. • Make sure young people have the right skills. • Make more apprenticeships available. • Provide more jobs for young people.	• Give schools and colleges money to provide courses in job skills. • Set up schemes that encourage schools and colleges to work closely with employers and provide training. • Give grants to firms and companies to set up apprenticeships. • Give employers tax breaks and financial benefits if they take on young people.

4 When you have agreed your policies, you have to convince other people that you are right. You have to plan your **campaign**.

  a Use the chart to write your **party manifesto**. This sets out the main things your party wants to do (aims) and how you are going to achieve them (policies).

  b Discuss how you can persuade other people to agree with your views.

  c Design campaign posters and put them up in the classroom.

  d Write a three-minute speech for the leader of the party to give to the whole class.

  e You could then hold an election to see which party has the best ideas (see page 100).

6.6 Political parties in the UK

We hear about the main political parties all the time because they are in the news: the Labour Party, the Conservative Party, and the Liberal Democrats. There are, however, many political parties that we hear less about. The following political parties all have Members of Parliament:

Other political parties have no Members of Parliament at the moment. Some of them are quite small. More than 100 political parties are registered. Look at the logos of just a few:

Activity

Split the class up into small groups. Use the internet to find out about these political parties. You can find a list of them on Wikipedia with links to the parties.

1 Some groups can find information about the main parties:
  - Who is the leader?
  - What are the names of other key people and what jobs do they do?
  - What are the main aims of the party?
  - What is in their party manifesto or what are the main things they want to see done?

  Other groups can find out similar, or any particularly interesting, information about one of the smaller parties. Some of the smaller parties present themselves in a very different way to the main parties or have very specific objectives.

2 When you have finished, each group should make a brief presentation about the party they have researched.

General elections

Political parties present their policies to the people of Britain in general elections. This is when the voters or 'electorate' choose the Members of Parliament (MPs) who are to represent them in Parliament in the House of Commons. Each MP represents the people who live in a particular area of the country called a constituency. The area of each constituency varies but it contains around 69,000 people. You do not have to belong to a party to become an MP. You can be an 'Independent'.

The political party that wins the majority of seats (has most MPs) in the House of Commons forms the government and runs the country.

A People in the past have fought for the right to vote and we should take our responsibility seriously. In some countries, people are not allowed to vote and have no way of changing or influencing their governments.

B All the main parties are the same. It does not make any difference who wins the elections.

C If you don't vote you can't complain about the government when it does things you don't like.

D MPs in Parliament make laws and decisions that affect our lives in a big way. We should take part in electing these MPs.

E Once MPs get elected, they don't listen to us and do what they want. So there is no point in voting.

F MPs are only out for their own personal gain, for money or for power and influence, so I won't vote for them.

G I don't understand what they are going on about and I am not that interested, so I won't bother to vote.

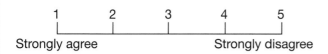

Activity

Why vote?

Some people don't bother to vote in general elections. In some countries, like Australia, it is compulsory to vote.

1 Look at the arguments (A to G). For each one, rank them on a scale 1–5 on how much you agree with them.

```
1       2       3       4       5
Strongly agree          Strongly disagree
```

2 Compare your rankings in class and discuss whether you think it is important to vote or not.

3 Do you think people should be made to vote and fined if they don't?

6.7 How do you become a Member of Parliament (MP)?

All citizens of the United Kingdom over the age of 18 are eligible for election to Parliament, unless they are, or have been, in prison, have certain kinds of mental illness or are members of the House of Lords. *You* could be an MP when you are older.

Activity

These pictures show the stages in becoming an MP but they are in the wrong order. Put them in the correct order and draw a flow chart to show how somebody becomes an MP. If there are any words you don't understand, you will find them explained in the Glossary starting on page 126.

A Anna Cassidy joins a political party. She works for the party, attending meetings, helping out at election time and raising funds.

C A general election is called. Anna and her supporters run a **campaign**. Party volunteers canvass for her; they knock on doors asking the voters to vote for Anna. They use posters, leaflets and public meetings to set out the ideas and policies of Anna and her party.

D The day of the election arrives. The voters go to a **polling station**. They are each given a **ballot paper** with the names of the candidates on it. They take their paper to a polling booth (where no-one can see what they are writing) and put an 'X' next to the candidate they want to vote for. Then they put their ballot paper in a sealed metal box.

B After the vote has ended, all the **ballot boxes** in the constituency are collected and the votes are counted. The **Returning Officer** then announces that Anna is the candidate with the most votes. She is now the MP for her constituency and will go to the House of Commons.

E Anna puts her name forward to be an MP. Along with several other people, she is interviewed by a selection committee. She is chosen to be her party's candidate at the next election.

First-past-the-post system

The system used in this country for parliamentary elections is called the first-past-the-post system. This means that the person who wins the most votes in a constituency is elected as the MP. Some people think this is the best system because:

- it is simple to understand.
- people know clearly who represents them in their area.
- it usually (but not always) creates a clear winner, with one party having the majority of MPs and this leads to strong government.

Other people think that this system is unfair because the votes of those who voted for other candidates are not taken into account. They would prefer a system called proportional representation (PR) where the seats in Parliament would be shared out by all the parties according to the total vote they received in the election. This system often leads to a coalition government (see the section on coalition governments below).

Activity

1 Look at the example in the table below.
   a Who won?
   b What percentage of people voted for this person?
   c What percentage did not vote for this person?
   d Do you think the result of the vote is fair for all voters?

Party	Eastside constituency	Westside constituency	Northside constituency	Southside constituency	Central constituency	Share of total vote
Union Party	500	400	400	200	500	2,000 (40%)
People's Party	400	390	610	400	200	2,000 (40%)
Planet Party	200	210	190	200	200	1,000 (20%)
The winning party is…						

Hung parliaments and coalition governments

If no one party has a majority in the House of Commons, it is called a **hung parliament**. This means that the government has to work with other parties to run the country. Sometimes two or more parties get together to form the government. This is called a **coalition government**. They have to agree policies the government is going to follow. Each party might then have to change its policies and ideas to fit in with the other.

Activity

Do you think coalition governments are a good idea because parties have to work with each other, or do you think it creates a weak government?

6.8 Should 16-year-olds be given the vote?

In the UK at present you have to be 18 to vote. However, there is an increasing number of people who think that the voting age should be lowered to 16. Do you think this is a good idea?

Activity

1 In pairs, read the statements below and on page 111 and decide whether you are for or against lowering the voting age to 16. Suggest some other reasons why 16-year-olds should or should not be able to vote.

2 Debate this in class. Arrange for people who take different sides to argue their case. See if anybody changes their mind.

3 Draw a small poster/ leaflet which is designed to encourage people to support or reject the idea of reducing the voting age to 16.

Or, design a poster/leaflet encouraging young people to vote as soon as they are able. This should include some of the arguments about why they should take an interest and vote in a general election.

A
Young people can get married and join the army at 16, so they should be able to vote.

B
You are not allowed to have a drink or see a horror film till you are 18, so how are you able to vote?

C
Most 16-year-olds are not grown up enough to vote.

D
Most 16-year-olds would probably just copy their parents or do the opposite to their parents, so they would not be voting for the right reasons.

E
Lots of 16-year-olds have strong views and know a lot about issues like education, climate change and housing. Many know more about things than older people. So they have just as much right to vote.

F
At 16 you can be working and paying tax. If you pay tax to the government, you should be able to vote about how it spends taxes.

G
Young people have been deeply affected by the economic crisis and the lack of jobs. They should be able to vote on the way the government is dealing with these issues.

H
Many young people feel they have been left out of society. Voting would be a good way to include them.

I
Eighteen is the right age for the vote. People have become much more mature in the two years after 16 and know a lot more about the world. Sixteen is too young.

J
Several countries have already reduced the voting age to 16.

Activity

Your class could hold an election to see how the first past the post system works. You could do this for a class election or you could do it following on from the Activity on page 105. Create a ballot paper like the one shown here.

Candidates	☒ Mark a cross against your chosen candidate
BROWN, Sam (Monster Raving Loony Party)	
JONES, Frankie (Conservative Party)	
MACDONALD, Angus (Independent)	
PATEL, Rehanna (Liberal Democrats)	
ROBERTS, Chris (Labour Party)	
SMITH, Alice (Green Party)	

6.9 What does an MP do?

In the House of Commons

Making laws
MPs play an important part in making laws in the House of Commons. They look carefully at the laws, debate them and suggest changes to them.

Representing people
An MP represents all the people in their constituency in the House of Commons, whether they voted for the MP or not. You can visit, write to or email your MP to make your views known. The MP can represent these views in the House of Commons.

Working on committees
Many MPs work on Select Committees which examine specific issues like transport or the environment. They research and discuss these issues so that they can report on them to the House of Commons.

Making speeches and taking part in debates
An MP takes part in debates and makes speeches.

Outside the House of Commons

Meeting constituents
An MP holds 'surgeries' in the local constituency to meet local people and discuss their problems or issues. An MP can play an important part in bringing different communities together.

Visits and fact-finding
An MP makes visits to places like schools, hospitals and day centres for old people. This can provide useful information about people's concerns to take back to Parliament. They might travel abroad to find out about international issues such as poverty, debt or women's rights around the world.

Activity

You can see that an MP's job is quite demanding. They need to have a wide range of skills and knowledge to be able to do it. In pairs, write a job description for a Member of Parliament which takes the things an MP has to do into account.

1 Use the information on the list to the right. Choose three qualities/abilities in each category (e.g. three from the skills category) that you think are most important for an MP to have.

2 Compare your final choices with others in the class and see if you agree/disagree.

3 Make a copy of the job description chart and complete it. You can add to your original choices if the class discussion has persuaded you that other qualities/skills are important.

Job description for the Member of Parliament for ……………………… constituency

You should have knowledge of …

The following skills will be very useful …

Useful experience would be …

You would possess some of the following personal qualities …

---

4 Find out:
   a who your MP is
   b the name of the constituency in which you live
   c how and when you could meet your MP.

5 Write a letter or email to your MP. He or she will usually have a website which tells you about them and what they are doing. Working with a partner, choose an issue you are interested in. This could be a local issue, such as safety on the streets, or a national or international issue like helping people in developing countries. In your letter or email, explain your views and ask for the MP's reaction.

Knowledge of:
- the local area
- how to get things done in the Party
- local issues
- national issues in the UK
- world issues
- how Parliament works.

Personal qualities
- honesty
- straightforwardness
- able to get on with all kinds of people
- cheerful and amusing
- can mix with people socially
- able to be positive at all times
- hard working
- perseverance
- dedicated.

Skills
- speaking in public
- being interviewed for television/radio
- fundraising
- negotiating
- chairing committees
- putting across a message
- managing a business.

Experience
- has run a business or organisation
- worked in a profession
- worked in campaigns
- married with children
- lived in local area for several years
- served as a local councillor.

3 Station Road
Sunnydale
Midshire
SU12 1PL

John Green MP
House of Commons
London
SW1A 0AA

Dear Mr Green,

I am sure you have heard that they are planning to close Littledeen Primary School. Everybody in our family and all our neighbours are very angry about this. It should be kept open because …

6.10 What's going on in the House of Commons?

The Prime Minister and the other members of the Government run the United Kingdom. But they can't just do what they want. They have to explain and account for their actions in the House of Commons. The Government needs the support of the House of Commons to pass laws. If a majority of MPs in the House regularly vote against the Government, the Government may have to resign.

What does the House of Commons do?

- It makes laws.
- It questions the Government and examines what it is doing.
- It keeps a check on the amount of money that the Government spends.
- It holds debates on issues of national importance.

Activity

1   Look at the outline drawing of the inside of the House of Commons. To learn about it, match the numbers 1–11 with one of the letters A–K on the opposite page. Some are straightforward, some you will have to work out.

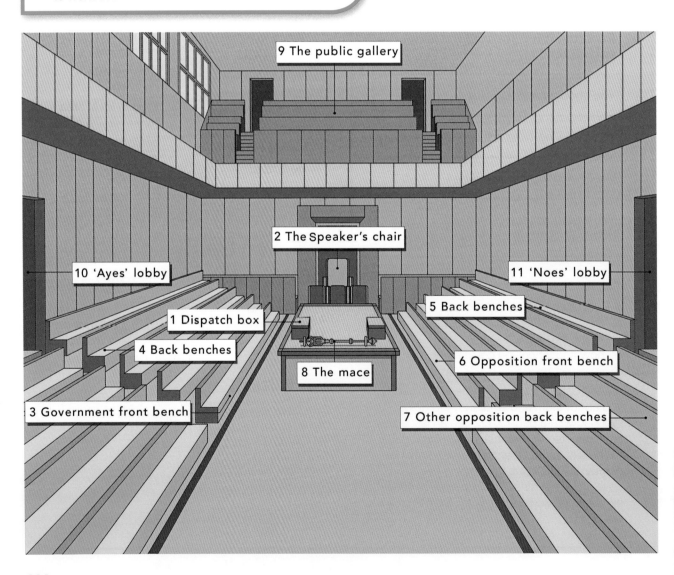

9 The public gallery
2 The Speaker's chair
10 'Ayes' lobby
11 'Noes' lobby
5 Back benches
1 Dispatch box
4 Back benches
6 Opposition front bench
8 The mace
3 Government front bench
7 Other opposition back benches

A
Government ministers and the Prime Minister sit here just behind the dispatch box.

F
The MPs from the political party (or parties) forming the Government sit behind the Government.

B
The leaders of the opposition sit on the front bench on the other side from the Government.

G
MPs go here when voting in favour of something.

C
This is the symbol to show the House of Commons is sitting.

H
The MPs who belong to the party of the Opposition sit on the opposite side of the House of Commons, facing the Government.

D
The Speaker runs debates, calls people to speak and keeps order in the House of Commons.

I
This is where MPs who belong to the other opposition parties sit.

E
The Prime Minister and ministers stand here to make announcements or answer questions.

J
MPs go here when they are voting against something.

K
This is where members of the public can sit to watch the proceedings in Parliament.

The Opposition

The party with the second largest number of MPs in the House of Commons forms the official Opposition. The job of the Opposition in the Commons is to challenge the Government, raise questions about the way it is running the country and make sure it is not corrupt. The Opposition sits on the front benches facing the Government.

Activity

2   You can find out a lot more about the Houses of Parliament and see it in action by going to www.parliament.uk/education

One of the main jobs of the House of Commons is to pass new laws, change ones that already exist and get rid of ones that no longer serve any useful purpose.

Stages in making a law

A proposed law is set out in what is called a 'Bill'.

1 **First reading** – the Bill is published for MPs to read. There is no discussion or vote.

2 **Second reading of the Bill** – a government minister explains the purpose of the Bill and answers questions about it. If a majority of MPs vote for it, it goes on to the next stage.

3 **Committee stage** – a small committee of MPs looks at the details of the Bill. It suggests changes or amendments to the Bill and votes on these.

4 **Report stage** – the committee reports to the House on the Bill. MPs can suggest further changes.

5 **Third reading** – this gives the House a chance to look at the whole Bill with amendments. After a debate, MPs vote for it or reject it.

6 **House of Lords** – the Bill goes to the Lords who check it. They may suggest changes which are discussed with the House of Commons but they cannot stop the Bill becoming law.

7 **The Royal Assent** – the Bill must be signed by the King or Queen before it becomes law.

8 **Act of Parliament** – the Bill is now a law.

A new Bill proposes that:

No animals should be used in any form of experimentation and testing.

Activity

1 Half the class will support the Bill and half oppose it. This means that you may have to argue for something that you do not believe in. It is important to do this sometimes to see an issue from a different point of view.

2 First, work in groups of three. Use some of the arguments below to develop your own ideas. You can research more arguments on the internet. Choose which one of your group is going to speak in the debate. This means that there should be three or four speakers for each side.

3 Hold the debate.

4 Each group of three can now suggest one amendment (change) to the Bill that they think is fair and good and would improve the Bill. For example, animals can be used for experiments that will help prevent diseases in human beings.

5 The class now votes on the whole Bill. If the majority vote for it, it becomes law.

Arguments

A Millions of animals are suffering intolerable cruelties. They are left blind, in pain and severely disturbed by the experiments to which they are subjected.

B There is simply no real alternative for experimentation on animals for testing the effects that a range of products and chemicals and drugs have on human beings.

C It is simple: animal testing saves human lives and protects us from the dangerous effects of all sorts of chemicals and drugs that make our lives better, whether this is in medicine or in the household products we use.

D There are plenty of alternatives to using animals. Modern science has come up with all sorts of ways for testing products and the effects of chemicals without using animals.

Possible amendments

- The use of animals for medical tests should be allowed.
- Tests for chemicals and products that are going into everyday use would be allowed.
- Tests should be allowed but the laboratories the animals are kept in would be strictly supervised and unnecessary cruelty outlawed.
- Scientists would have to show that tests on animals are essential and that there are no real alternatives before being allowed.

E Why should human beings benefit at the cost of animals? They share the earth with us and should have equal respect.

F If you stopped tests with animals, medical progress would be held back and it would take a lot longer to find cures for many diseases and conditions.

6.12 How should the House of Lords be modernised?

The House of Lords is the second house in the British Parliament. It is not elected like the House of Commons, which is by far the more powerful House. The 'Lords' can delay laws being passed but the 'Commons' can force laws through.

Who's in the House of Lords?

There are around 800 members (called 'peers') who have seats in the House of Lords. They are made up of:

Life peers

These are appointed for life. They usually have expertise in areas like the sciences, arts, religion or business. Some are given peerages for service to a political party, e.g. ex-MPs.

Hereditary peers

Originally, the 'Lords' was mostly made up of the most important lords, barons and earls. Their right to be in the 'Lords' was passed down to their heirs and so many 'peers' inherited their seats. Many people felt it was wrong that members of certain families should, by right of birth, have influential positions in the British Parliament. So, in 1999, most hereditary peers had their seats removed, although 92 were elected to stay.

Bishops

There are 26 Church of England Bishops who sit in the 'Lords'.

What does the House of Lords do?

The main jobs are to:

- act as a check on the 'Commons' to make sure that new laws are discussed thoroughly and not rushed through
- look critically at the work of the Government
- hold debates on important issues which may influence the Government and the 'Commons'.

How would you modernise it?

Some people would like to get rid of the House of Lords altogether. They say that the House of Commons, which is elected, can do all the work that is needed. But others say it is important to have a second House act as a check and balance to the Government and the 'Commons'. Also, it is very useful to have people with lots of experience in different areas helping to make laws and advising the Government. Some people think it would be best if it represented different UK regions more strongly, so people could speak up for the south-west or the north-east.

Activity

Working in groups, decide how you would make the House of Lords more modern by working through the sections below. Then compare your decisions with other groups and explain why you made the choices you did.

1 What would you call it?

  a the House of Lords
  b the Second House
  c the Senate
  d some other name – you choose

2 Would you elect or appoint? Would:

  a 100% be elected by voters?
  b 75% elected and 25% appointed?
  c 50% elected and 50% appointed?
  d 100% appointed?

3 How long should people stay in the House?

  a for life
  b five years for those who are elected, ten if appointed
  c a different amount of time for elected and appointed members (you decide)
  d elections and appointments to take place at same time as a General Election

4 The members of the House should largely be made up of (you can choose more than one option)?

  a older experienced people from different areas of expertise, e.g. scientists, lawyers, teachers, doctors, religious leaders, business people, others (you decide)
  b a minimum percentage of women and ethnic minorities (you decide what percentage)
  c a mix of young and older people
  d people who represent the different regions of the UK

5 What power should the House have?

  a the power to reject Bills passed in the Commons
  b similar powers to the existing House of Lords
  c the power to advise and suggest changes to Bills
  d some other powers that you decide

Some thoughts to bear in mind

If the House was 100% elected then:

- It could challenge the House of Commons and this might lead to problems and delays.
- You would not necessarily have a range of people in the House.
- The same parties would dominate and it would not be much different from the House of Commons.

If the House has too much power, it could:

- stop laws going through
- interfere with the government running the country.

6.13 Influencing government: pressure groups and lobbying

Many people wish to influence government decisions in-between elections. For many people, a vote every five years is not enough, especially when they have strong views on specific issues or areas of life. In this topic, we are going to look at the various methods used to influence government policies in our democracy and consider whether these methods are fair and equally available for everyone to use.

Pressure groups

Some people get together to form pressure groups to make sure their views are heard and taken into account by government ministers, peers and MPs. Sometimes they are fighting for their own interests or rights; sometimes they are fighting for the rights of others or promoting a cause. Pressure groups from different sides of the same issue often oppose each other and compete to get their views heard by decision-makers.

An example of this is the debate about plain packaging for cigarettes. Some pressure groups, for example, the BMA (British Medical Association), argue that unbranded packaging makes cigarettes less appealing to smokers and would prevent young people taking up smoking, while Forest (a smokers' support group) and the tobacco industry say the evidence is not conclusive, and that plain packaging will lose them money and therefore cut jobs.

Greenpeace
▲ Aims to defend the natural world, protect the environment and promote peace

Royal Society for the Prevention of Cruelty to Animals (RSPCA)

The Law Society
▲ Represents and protects solicitors in England and Wales

Surfers Against Sewage

Amnesty International
▲ Aims to uncover and stop abuses of human rights across the world

Countryside Alliance
▲ Campaigns on issues to do with the countryside and gives people in rural areas a voice

Road Haulage Association
▲ Represents the interests of road haulage (lorry and truck) operators

Plane Stupid
▲ Campaigns against the expansion of the aviation (airplanes), especially airports which affect people's lives

Confederation of British Industry (CBI)
▲ Provides a voice for employers at national level, lobbies government on behalf of businesses

Activity

1 On this page and opposite are more examples of pressure groups. Which out of these organisations do you think are fighting for their own interests and which are fighting for the interests of others or promoting a cause?

2 What other pressure groups have you heard of?

3 Choose one of the pressure groups on these pages, or one of your own choice, to research on the internet. Find out particularly about their aims, methods or campaign tactics and what they have achieved. Present your findings to the rest of the class.

4 Some groups organise events and campaigns to get the public on their side, using the methods described on pages 88–89. Which of these were used by the pressure group you researched?

Fathers4Justice

▲ Fights for the rights of fathers to have access to, and develop relationships with, their children after family break-ups

Age UK

▲ To inspire, enable and support older people to help people make the most of later life

National Society for the Prevention of Cruelty to Children

Liberty

▲ Fights for civil liberties and human rights for everyone

National Union of Teachers

Campaign for Nuclear Disarmament (CND)

▲ Campaigns to scrap nuclear weapons

Christian Aid

▲ Aims to change the world to one where everyone can live a full life, free from poverty

Taxpayers' Alliance

▲ Campaigns for lower taxes and reduction in public spending

Pro-Test

▲ Supports animal testing in medical experiments which benefit human beings

Lobbying

Some people try to influence decision-makers by privately meeting powerful people, sending them information or inviting them to presentations. This is called lobbying and is carried out by individual members of the public, groups of constituents or organised pressure groups. There are also some professional lobbying organisations, who agree to influence powerful decision-makers for a fee.

MPs and members of the House of Lords are the target of many different lobbying interests. Often these lobbyists hope to get the MP or peer to vote a certain way on a specific issue. However, this decision should be down to the MP or the peer's own judgement and their political party policy.

Anyone can lobby their MP – it is one of the rights of individuals in our democracy. You write to him/her and arrange a meeting, originally held in the lobby of the Houses of Parliament, which is where the name comes from.

Recently, there has been concern that professional lobby groups have too much influence over members of the Houses of Parliament. There are three main worries:

● The size of the lobbying industry – there are many hundreds of organisations willing to push a particular view on behalf of clients for a fee.
● The kinds of clients – these are often big global businesses which have lots of money to be made, or lost, from government decisions and policies, and can afford to pay lobbyists.
● The methods used by lobbyists – sometimes in the past, they have used shady methods. There have been cases in the past of MPs taking 'cash for questions', i.e. agreeing to ask a question in one of the Houses of Parliament for money. Also, there have been cases of 'cash for access', i.e. lobbyists claiming to have close contacts with government ministers and offering to put a case, again for money.

Activity

Lobbying Members of Parliament and the Lords is an important right in our democracy. If you were in government, how would you make sure that every-one had equal access to decision-makers in the Houses of Parliament?

Think about:
● whether money should change hands
● how everyone can get access to important people
● how more people can gain knowledge of the system
● how everyone can have more confidence to approach decision-makers.

Internet campaigns

With the popularity of digital technology, many pressure group campaigns have gone online and use email, blogs, Facebook and Twitter to promote their causes.

38 Degrees is an example of a campaigning group that attracts thousands of people to support various campaigns, using email voting and electronic petitions.

38 Degrees is not the only campaigning group that makes use of the internet to get support for an issue. Many pressure groups now urge supporters to flood their MPs with email messages and online petitions on specific issues, and it seems to be working. MPs, both in government and opposition, are feeling that matters are being taken out of their hands. Email campaigners are often referred to as 'clicktivists'.

Activity

Look at the arguments expressed below and on page 123 and decide which ones are FOR electronic campaigning and which are AGAINST. Compare your answers with a partner.

'38 Degrees is the angle at which an avalanche happens. In the UK, 38 Degrees will enable people to act together, to create an avalanche for change.'

The organisation claims to bring people together to take action on the issues that matter to them. It is a broad organisation which does not focus on one issue, but allows people signed up by email to vote on the issues they feel strongly about. Examples of some issues it has campaigned on include the National Health Service, climate change and press abuses.

It is too easy to encourage people to click on a link and sign a petition or send an email without having to think too deeply about the issue and finding things out for themselves.

Email campaigns are true democracy because everyone can be involved and their voices heard, even if they are very busy and don't usually follow politics closely.

Email campaigns sidestep the long-standing political process of trusting the locally elected MP to speak up for people's views in Parliament.

People have lost faith in their MPs to truly represent them and they want their voices heard directly.

Online petitions and email campaigns are not a true reflection of public opinion because they can be signed several times by the same person.

Email campaigns are more likely to engage younger people who may not have shown much interest in politics in the past.

Poorer and older people in our society are less likely to have access to the internet and so their voices will be crowded out by those who own computers, tablets and smartphones.

Activity

Get your views heard

You might feel strongly about something going on in your local community, such as the lack of facilities for young people, or something going on in your school. Plan a campaign to get your views heard.

1 Decide on the campaign issue and carry out some research to find out who the decision-makers are and what the arguments are surrounding the issue.

2 Create your own pressure group of people who share your views.

3 Decide what tactics/methods you intend to use to raise public awareness and get people on your side (e.g. posters, website, online petition, organised event).

4 Target the local decision-makers that you might need to lobby (e.g. councillors, MP, headteacher). Decide which media outlets (newspapers, local radio station, etc.) you would contact and how you would get them interested in your campaign.

5 Do it!

6 Review your action: what worked and what didn't? What would you change to improve future campaigns?

The Government makes decisions about how the country is run and how things get done, for example, building more schools and hospitals, fighting wars and creating new jobs. It has an army of civil servants to put these decisions into action (see page 102).

You're in the Cabinet!

The Cabinet is the top government committee. It meets regularly and is chaired by the Prime Minister. Its members have to agree to support the policies the Government decides to adopt. This is called **collective responsibility** – all of them are responsible for the Government's actions.

There are usually between 20 and 22 members in the Cabinet. You can see some of the key members and the main things they are responsible for in the illustration below.

Unfortunately, there is never enough money to pay for all the things the Government wants to do. If one department wants more money, another has to lose it. Ministers have to argue in Cabinet for the money they need for their departments.

A country needs a government to:

- protect citizens and keep them safe
- look after their welfare
- run the economy
- look after the environment.

Minister for Education
Responsible for education and child protection

Minister for Transport
Responsible for roads, railways and air travel and safety

Foreign Secretary
Speaks for the UK in its dealings with other countries

Minister for Welfare and Employment
Responsible for benefits of all kinds and pensions

Prime Minister
Head of the Government and key decision-maker

Minister for the Environment
Responsible for looking after the environment, climate change measures and reducing pollution

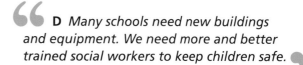
A *I need a bigger share of the money available for building new hospitals and training a thousand more nurses. We need new scanning equipment that will spot brain diseases earlier and save hundreds of lives.*

B *We have to build more roads for the increasing amount of traffic. The railways also need investment in high-speed lines.*

C *Reports have shown that our prisons are in a poor state. Millions of pounds need to be spent on them.*

D *Many schools need new buildings and equipment. We need more and better trained social workers to keep children safe.*

E *Time is running out for the environment with climate change accelerating. We have to build green sources of energy (using wind and wave power) and practise energy-saving in homes.*

F *We have already cut our armed forces significantly. If we don't spend more money on better equipment to protect our troops, new weapons and planes, we will not be able to fight a modern war or defend ourselves.*

G *More money is required to re-train people so they can find new jobs. We can't cut welfare benefits, such as housing and disability allowances, any more, and we have to pay for a new IT system to manage the payments of benefits generally.*

Minister for Defence
Responsible for the defence of the country and the armed forces

Home Secretary
Responsible for running the police force and the prisons, law and order and the justice system

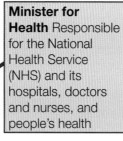

Minister for Health Responsible for the National Health Service (NHS) and its hospitals, doctors and nurses, and people's health

Chancellor of the Exchequer
Responsible for managing the finances of the Government – how much is spent and how much is collected in taxes – and for preparing the budget.

Activity

Form small groups of four or five. You are mini Cabinets. The Prime Minister has announced that government spending has to be cut and there is less money to go around. Seven ministers are arguing for more money for their departments.

1   Match the statements A to G with the ministers in the illustration.

2   Only four of the ministers can get more money, three will have to lose out. Decide which four are going to win and which three lose. Everybody in your group has to agree your final choice and take responsibility for the decisions, as a Cabinet would. You have to be able to give good reasons why you chose to give money to some and not other departments.

Glossary

Active citizen someone who wants to change things for the better, who is prepared to argue for and take action to change things or resist an unwanted change

Authoritarian enforcing strict control; obedience to authority as opposed to individual freedom

Ballot box where ballot papers are put

Ballot paper paper with the names of all the candidates who want to be elected. Voters choose one by putting a cross next to the appropriate name

Budget a plan showing income (money coming in) and expenditure (money spent which allows you to work out how much money you will need or are able to spend

Campaign the activities that candidates and their supporters undertake to persuade people to vote for them

Candidate person standing for election or applying for a job

Cash card a plastic card that allows you to withdraw cash from an ATM (cash machine)

Censorship banning or changing material (newspaper articles, books, films) to prevent it being seen by the public

Cheque a written instruction (usually on a pre-printed piece of paper) for money to be paid from one bank account to another person or organisation

Civil liberties the right to freedom of speech and action

Coalition government where two or more political parties form a government to run a country

Collective responsibility a whole group taking responsibility for the decisions its members make or the actions they take

Community a group of people who live near each other in a local area; a group of people who share common beliefs or ways of life

Constituency the voters in a particular area who elect an MP to Parliament

Consumer a person who buys goods and services

Court a place where a judge or magistrate tries cases and sentences those found guilty

Credit card a plastic card that allows you buy things now and pay for them later. You may have to pay interest on the purchases

Current account a bank account that you can pay money into or take money out of at any time

Debit card a plastic card that allows you to pay goods and services in shops or online without the need to use cash. The money is taken directly from your account

Democracy a system of government where people regularly elect their leaders and have a say in the way a country is governed

Despotic the adjective of the noun, 'despot', which means a 'tyrannical ruler'

Direct action action taken where the normal channels are regarded as too slow or ineffective, often some sort of disruptive activity, legal or illegal, to arouse public awareness or achieve an objective

Discrimination treating someone unfairly as a result of prejudice

Election a way of choosing someone for a particular position by voting

Electorate all the people who can vote in an election

Equal opportunities getting a fair chance, regardless of gender, race, religion or other beliefs, to receive an education, get a job and promotion, obtain housing, etc.

Fairness treating people in a just, unbiased way

Freedom the right to act, think or speak as you want, without interference from a despotic government

Hire purchase (HP) an arrangement to buy goods in instalments over a period of time. You don't own the goods until you have paid off the total sum and there are often conditions which apply to the arrangement

Human rights rights that are held to belong to any person. The United Nations Universal Declaration of Human Rights, 1948, sets out a full list of the rights that all people should have

Hung parliament where no party has a clear majority and has to rely on the support of other parties to win votes in parliament

Interest the sum of money you are given as a reward for saving with a bank or building society, or the money you are charged by an organisation/person which is lending you money. It is usually shown as a percentage, e.g. 5%

Justice the administration of the law according to accepted principles

Law a rule that has the backing of the government

Legal system the processes and institutions that make and uphold our laws

Loan a sum of money you borrow from a person/ organisation that you have to pay back over a period of time, usually with interest added

Magistrate a member of the local community who deals with cases that are brought before magistrates' and youth courts

Manifesto a statement of policies and aims

Member of Parliament (MP) someone who is elected to sit in Parliament to represent the people who voted for them

Monarchy a system of government in which a king or queen plays an important part in running a country

Offender someone who has broken the law

Opinion what someone thinks about a particular issue; not a fact

Overdraft when you have no money in your bank account but continue to take money out of it with or without the bank's agreement

Parliament the place where people meet to discuss important issues, make laws and question the government about the way it is running the country

Party manifesto a statement of the party's aims and policies

PIN – Personal Identification Number a security number which you have to type in when using a debit card or cash card at a bank or cash machine

Policies courses of action that people plan to carry out or are in the process of carrying out

Political party an organised group of people who share a particular set of values, views and objectives and who put forward people to stand in elections

Polling station the place where the voters cast their votes, usually a school or a church hall

Prejudice opinions that we form without knowing all the facts or much information

Pressure group an organisation that has strong opinions on a particular issue and attempts to influence the people who make decisions

Proportional representation an electoral system in which the number of seats a party gets is in proportion to the number of votes it receives

Protest a public show of disagreement

Republic a system of government where the people or their elected representatives hold power rather than a monarch. Usually, the head of state is called the president

Responsibility recognising what you owe to other people in your community; acting towards other people in a caring or thoughtful way; being accountable for your own actions

Returning Officer the person who is in charge of counting the votes in a constituency and declares who the winner is after the count

Rights how a person expects or wants to be treated by others

Rules the code of behaviour that is laid down in a group or organisation, which everyone is expected to obey

Sentence the punishment given to a person who has been found guilty in a court

Sovereignty the authority of a state to exercise power, to make laws and run its own affairs

Store card a plastic card supplied by a retail outlet (e.g. a store) which allows cashless payments to buy goods in the store or online. It works like a credit card but only in a particular store or chain of stores

Surveillance being watched; observing the behaviour of people especially by government organisations

Tax money paid by individuals and companies to the government